Tattoo Meanings & Tattoo Design Symbolism

GRAHAME DAVID GARLICK

ISBN-13: 978-1506107561
ISBN-10: 1506107567

CONTENTS

GRAHAME DAVID GARLICK

1. ALL SEEING EYES

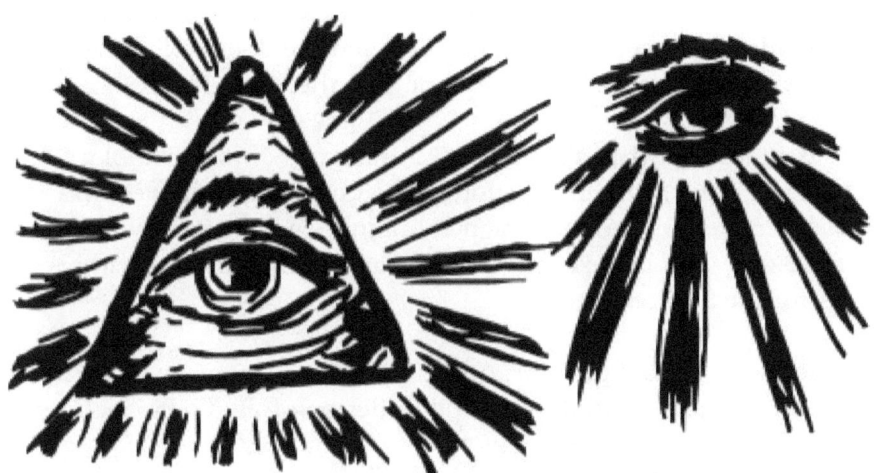

The all seeing eye is an extremely popular tattoo design at the moment, particularly among neo-traditional enthusiasts. The typical all seeing eye design is simply an eye in a triangle. For most people this imagery instantly brings to mind freemasonry, there is however many different meanings this symbol can carry.

If you are an American or have ever seen an American dollar bill then you will have probably noticed the Eye of Providence sat atop a pyramid printed on the reverse. This is again, an eye in a triangle. The Eye of Providence on the dollar bill is actually depicting the all-seeing eye of God and is surrounded by rays of light or "glory". You may also notice the pyramid on the dollar bill that the eye sits atop of has 13 layers, this is often mentioned by conspiracy theorists and given a darker meaning. The actual reason for the 13 layers is to represent the 13 original states.

Now to the Freemasons. The Eye of Providence was first used as part of the iconography of the Freemasons in 1797. This is thought to be a reminder to the masons that they were always being watched by God who, in Masonry is known as "The Great Architect of the Universe". The main difference in the design with regards to Freemasonry is that the rays of light or "glory" is depicted in a semicircular fashion around the bottom of the eye and is not always enclosed in a triangle.

A popular conspiracy theory surrounding the design is that the Eye of Providence is used on the Great Seal and the dollar bill because Masons were influential in the founding of the United States.

This is simply not true, the earliest Masonic use of the symbol was actually 14 years after the creation of the Great Seal. The Seal was actually created by various design committees whose members were not Masons, with the exception of Benjamin Franklin who had his ideas for the Seal rejected.

Furthermore, several Masonic organizations have gone so far as to deny any connection to the creation or design of the Great Seal.

So in conclusion, the links between the design and the Freemasons seem to be valid in that they did use an all seeing eye as part of their imagery and still do to this day. However the imagery was used simply to remind them that god is watching over them, the same reason it was used on the Great Seal.

So this is really a religious tattoo that pays homage to God, despite the folk lore surrounding it and claims that it may be in fact a satanic symbol. I would be wary however if you are a thinking of getting this design tattooed as a lot of people will probably think that it is Masonic and ask you why you got it. But then again you can just hit them with the information you just learned here and you will be fine!

2. ANCHORS

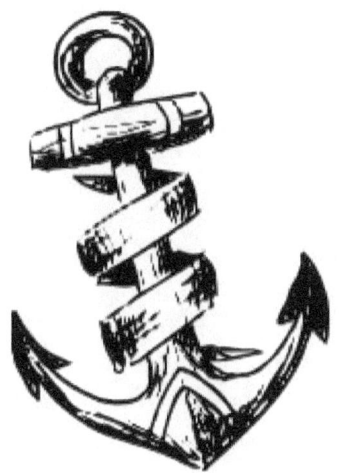 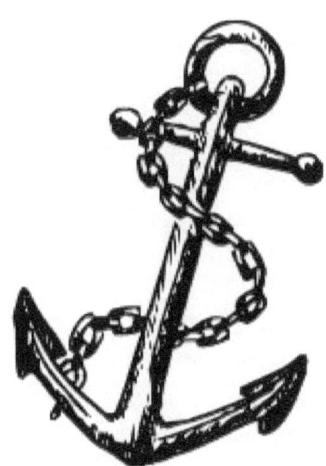

The anchor tattoo originated with the advent of electric tattooing, when sailors would travel from port to port and would get a tattoo to represent the life they led. The reason for the popularity among sailors and navy personnel is self-explanatory but we can find a lot more symbolism in the anchor design than you may have first thought.

The most common meaning associated with anchor tattoos is when someone feels as if they have found the place where they want to be in life. They may get an anchor tattoo to symbolize they have found where they want to "drop anchor".

The opposite meaning can also be true of anchors. A rising anchor can symbolize hope, a new chapter or a new adventure. Just like a ship raising its anchor when it is about to set sail on a new voyage. This can also symbolize hope and heading in the unknown.

The anchor is also a powerful symbol of steadfastness. Anchors are obviously meant to keep a ship anchored in place even in rough seas so they have to be strong and steadfast.

This can be an excellent metaphor to symbolize a time when you have made a stand or set yourself a challenge or new set of rules to stick to. The metaphor extends to how the rough seas will try to move an anchored ship but the anchor holds it steady through the storm. No matter how rough things get the anchor is a symbol of not giving up on your new challenge.

Anchors are also sometimes tied in with Christianity. The top section of an anchor usually looks like the crucifix symbol and is therefore associated with sacrifice and salvation. I have heard that in Roman times for example, Christians would have an anchor tattoo to let other Christians know who they were without drawing attention to themselves.

I think overall an anchor tattoo is perfect for symbolizing a significant stage in your life whether you are setting off on a new adventure, setting a new challenge to stick to or anchoring yourself down for a more settled stage in your life.

3. ANGELS

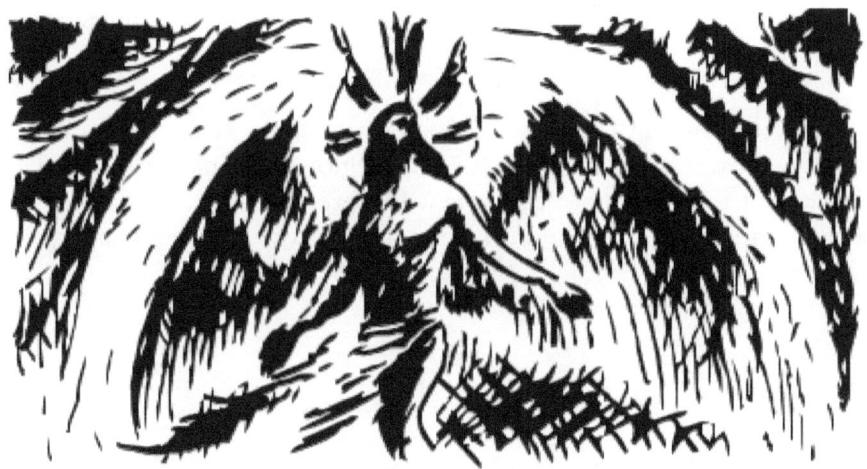

Angels symbolize the connection between heaven and earth as they are traditionally viewed as messengers from heaven.

Angels can also hold meaning as a tribute or a memorial tattoo for a loved one who has passed away. The symbolism behind this type of tattoo is that angels protect and guide our souls as they pass into heaven.

Angels are also symbolic of acts of great strength and courage. In historical works of art angels have often been depicted fighting in great battles. The angel Michael for example is a symbol of the ultimate warrior, this type of tattoo is perfect for showing spiritual strength.

Guardian angels are another popular meaning for tattoos. Having a guardian angel tattoo can symbolize a feeling of having a higher power watching over you and protecting you.

Angel tattoos are also excellent for showing faith. Angels are watchers, they observe and watch over us tirelessly, this makes their symbolism perfect for showing your unwavering faith. This can also be relevant for parents who may get an angel tattoo to reinforce in their mind that their job is to always watch over and protect their children on their journey through life.

Aside from this angels also represent divinity, awareness, innocence and purity.

Angel tattoos aren't for everyone, obviously if you aren't particularly religious or don't believe in organized religion then maybe an angel tattoo isn't for you as most people will more than likely automatically see you as being very religious if they see that you have an angel tattoo.

4. BATS

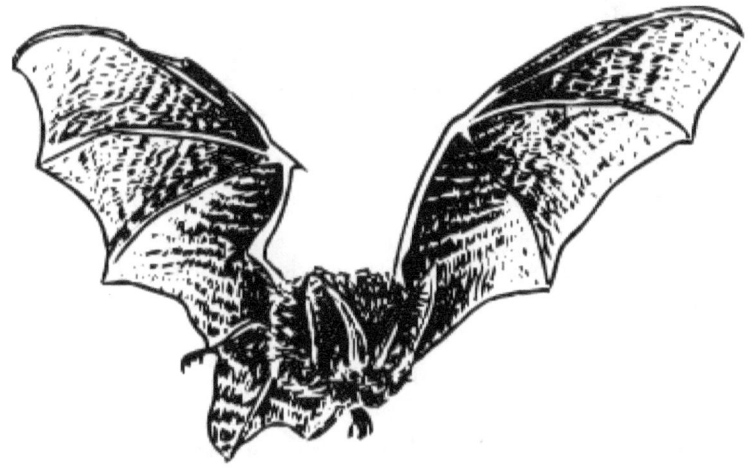

You may think of bats as being associated with dark scary caves and Halloween but there is a surprising amount of meaning and symbolism that can be associated with the humble bat.

Bats are extremely sensitive to their surroundings and can be a symbol of intuition, dreaming and vision. Native American shamans considered the bat to personify these qualities and became a powerful symbol in their culture.

Although they may not have fully understood the bats sonar like capabilities they did know that they were creatures of the night and that they had exceptionally good night vision. This made them symbols of foresight, being able to see through illusions and find the truth.

Bats are also highly social creates and are very nurturing to their young. They show signs of verbal communication and sensitivity with the other members of their colony. This surprising fact means that a bat tattoo could even be considered a tattoo symbolizing strong family ties.

Obviously there is a bit of an elephant in the room, vampire bats right? Don't bats hang out with vampires too? Well medieval texts written on the act of witchcraft, which they firmly believed in back then, did mention that bats are associated with witches and European medieval texts also linked them with vampires. The strange thing about this is that the vampire bat that we all know and love wasn't even discovered at this point in history due to South America not being explored yet. So yes, according to folklore the association is there. But then frogs and cats were also put in the same category as bats and we don't find them scary, well most of us don't.

In China however, bats are actually considered a symbol of luck and good fortune. In fact pretty much everywhere else in the world other than Europe, bats are considered to be pretty nice, interesting little creatures that not that scary at all really.

I will say though that if you do decide to get a bat tattoo, be prepared for some people to think you're a goth or biker who hangs out with the coven on weekends due to the common use of bat imagery by alternative subcultures.

Also the devil, dragons and other kinds of satanic or evil creates are all too often portrayed with bat like wings so there's always that too. If you're unsure, then it might be best to stay away from bat tattoos, but I think they have gotten a bit of a bad rap personally.

5. BUTTERFLIES

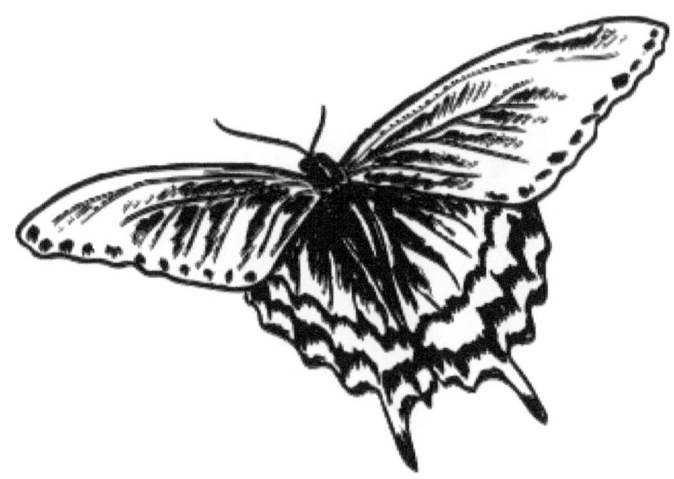

Perhaps predictably, the butterfly is a symbol of transformation. This can represent any kind of transformation in your life much as moving to a new area, a new lifestyle etc.

Butterfly tattoos can also represent the constant, gradual growth and changes that we all go through in our lives. Things that we may not even notice happening. So they don't necessarily have to directly relate to a specific event.

In many countries the butterfly is considered a symbol for the soul. In China it was believed to represent immortality and in Japan a white butterfly represented the soul of anyone whether they be living, dying or dead. In Greece butterflies also represented the soul and the immortality of the soul.

There is an old superstition in Japan that says if a butterfly enters your guest room and lands behind the bamboo screen, someone you love is coming to see you. So combine a butterfly with bamboo in a tattoo and hey presto, you have a cool story to tell people and a nice meaning to your tattoo.

Butterflies are of course a more feminine tattoo. For the guys out there looking for this type of symbolism, or girls that don't want a butterfly tattoo, moths can also represent similar qualities.

For more information on Moth symbolism there is a chapter later in the book.

6. CELTIC

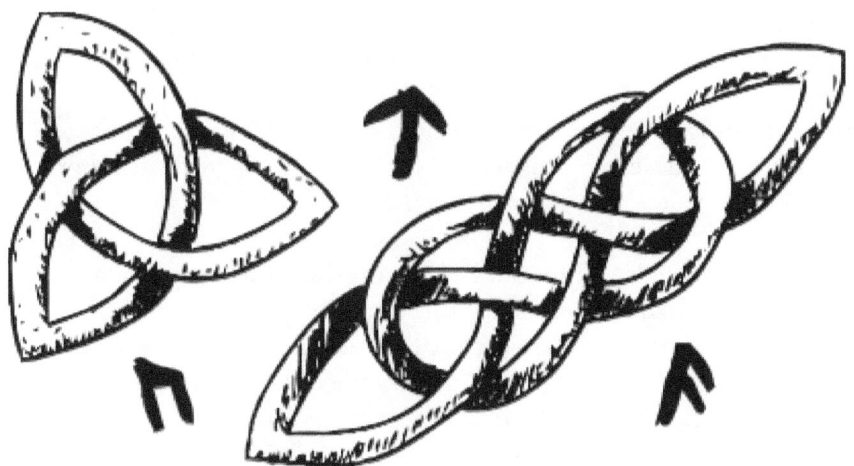

Celtic tattoos were very much a part of the Celtic warrior culture. The Picts (named after the latin Picti meaning "painted ones") would adorn themselves with tattoos to make themselves a more formidable sight for their enemies. The Celtic tribes would have adopted a similar style.

They fought with little or no armor, with dyed and spiked hair. Combine this with the tattoos and the fact they're a big hairy barbarian and you have something that you definitely would not want to mess with.

The tattoos were carried out using the Woad plant. The leaves were boiled, strained and reduced into a sort of primitive ink. This was then tapped into the skin using needle like objects creating a blue tattoo.

There were various types of imagery used for these tattoos. Rune like symbols were common among the warriors as they believed the symbols to carry various spell like powers when tattooed such as strength or protection.

Celtic knots were also commonplace and would often be tattooed on the arms and chest area.

Animal designs were also popular and carried much meaning. Animal designs were probably also worn by the warriors as they were believed to symbolize the strengths of the various animals.

There is a host of other Celtic designs such as crosses, La Tene, trinities, etc. These symbols would each have their own meaning, probably to reflect nature or the elements.

There has been a lot of research done on the various meanings of certain symbols and designs, far too much to go into in this book. If you are considering a Celtic design I would definitely recommend either getting a specialist book on the subject or doing some thorough research online before committing it to skin.

7. CHERRY BLOSSOMS

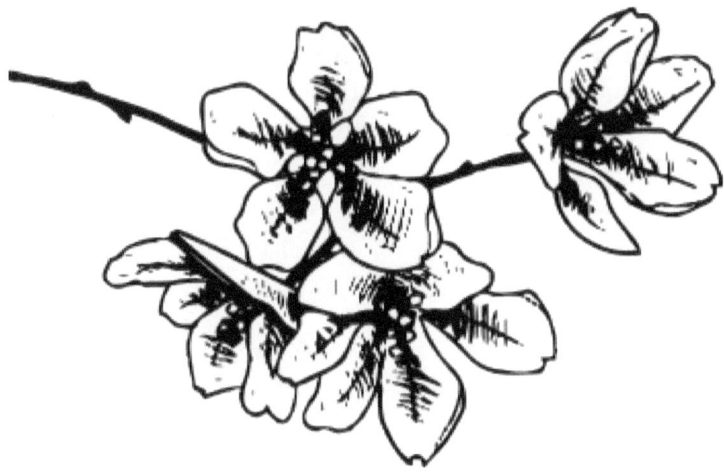

Cherry blossoms are known for blooming and falling in a short space of time. Because of this the Japanese view cherry blossoms as being a symbol of life.

Cherry blossoms serve as a reminder that life is fleeting and to make the most of the time we are given.

The Buddhist meaning is similar to this. As Buddhists believe we should exist in the moment and that we should remind ourselves every day that we are only here for a short time. So for Buddhists the cherry blossom is a powerful symbol.

In Japan the cherry blossom is so important that they have a yearly festival called hanami where thousands of people arrive to feast under the cherry blossom trees for the short time that they are in bloom.

This festival also takes place in New York since Japan gave 3000 cherry blossom trees to the US as a gift to reinforce the growing friendship between the two countries.

Cherry blossoms have a firm place in Japanese history as a symbol of nationalism. A fallen cherry blossom for example represents a fallen samurai. Because of this, during World War II, cherry blossoms were painted on the sides of the kamikaze planes.

Cherry blossoms can easily be incorporated into a sleeve or larger tattoo or as a standalone tattoo. Full branches are often combined with other things such as birds or butterflies to create great looking pieces of artwork.

8. CLOCKS & WATCHES

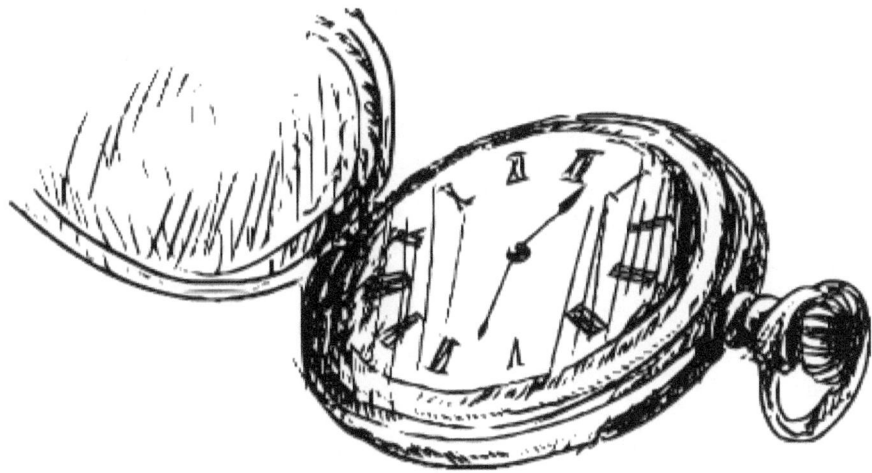

Clocks and watches are fairly popular tattoo designs at the moment, particularly vintage style grandfather clocks and pocket watches. There is a huge variety of designs and styles to choose from.

Originally clock tattoos were popular among prison inmates. They were often tattooed without hands and used to symbolize the time they spent on the inside.

Now clock and watch tattoos are no longer commonly linked to prison tattoos and have a far more pleasant meaning. The most obvious meaning of these types of tattoos is to represent time.

Clock tattoos are commonly associated with life and death and remembering that time doesn't stand still for anyone.

These tattoos can hold meaning in the same way as cherry blossoms for example, by reminding us that we have a certain amount of time and to use it wisely. Or to take opportunities and live our lives to the fullest.

Clock and watch tattoos can also be used as a memorial tattoo or as a reminder of a certain time that is significant to you. For example the exact birth time of a child could be recorded on the face of the clock.

Something to keep in mind is that due to the fine detail required, clock tattoos usually look better when tattooed bigger. Also you have to remember to keep in mind how your tattoo will age. All that fine detail done on a small tattoo will fade much quicker than on a larger tattoo where the detail can be enlarged.

9. COBWEBS

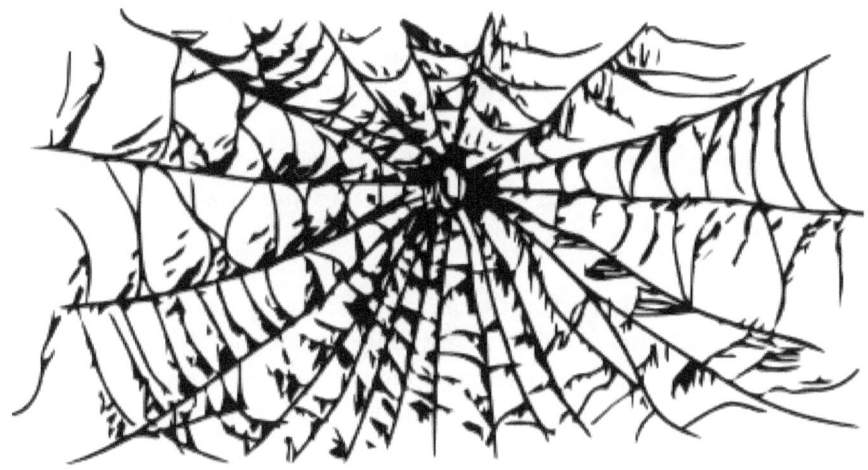

Cobweb tattoos are now generally just a fashionable tattoo usually tattooed around the elbow and little thought is given to their meaning and history.

Cobweb tattoos main meaning is to represent struggle. This is obviously due to the way spiders trap their prey in a web and how they struggle to escape it.

The stands of the web design also bare a resemblance to prison bars making them a popular tattoo among prison inmates. Both due to the jail cell bar symbolism and due to the metaphor of feeling trapped and the struggle to escape.

It has been said that the amount of rings on the web can represent the number of years and inmate spent on the inside. In some cases the rings may have indicated how many "victims" they had ensnared.

For the non-incarcerated tattoo aficionado however, these meanings can be representative of other struggles and the feeling of being trapped although not necessarily behind bars.

For example, feeling trapped by modern society and rules or the struggle against various difficulties you may have had in your life such as alcoholism for example.

Another thing to note is that another meaning connected to spider web tattoos is that a web on the left elbow indicates that the wearer is in possession of a hidden weapon.

Now it's time to get into the inevitable connection that spider web tattoos have with racism. It is true that white Supremacy groups would get webs tattooed to show their beliefs.

This has long since been forgotten however and getting a cobweb tattoo now would not be seen as anything out of the ordinary. So don't worry about being labeled as a racist by the vast majority of people. You may get the odd person telling you that it's racist and trying to look knowledgeable but you can just tell them it's far more likely to mean that you've been behind bars if anything!

10. COMPASSES

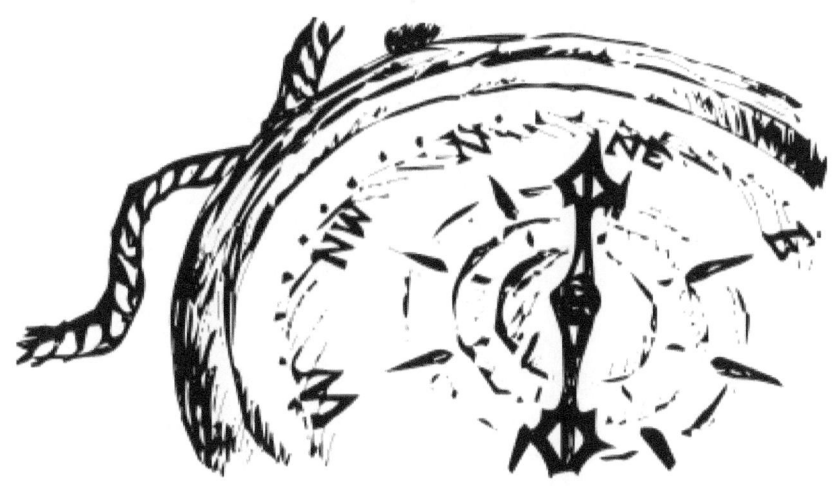

As I'm sure we all know, a compass is a navigational tool used to find magnetic north. A simple invention, with a highly scientific explanation behind its function.

The compass became an invaluable tool for sailors trying to navigate the open water. With no landmarks and just the sun and stars to guide them, sailing across a sea was not a task for the feint hearted to say the least! But with the invention of the compass that all changed overnight.

It's not too surprising then that reportedly the first compass tattoos can be traced back as far as the Spanish conquistadors, who were among the first to explore the new world of America when it was first discovered by the European nations.

The compass tattoo would also be found adorning the bodies of sailors and navy servicemen in the 1900s. The meaning behind the compass tattoo for these men was simple, it was a memento of their time spent at sea. Therefore one meaning for the compass tattoo can be a love for the sea, sailing, traveling etc.

The most popular meaning associated with compass tattoos in recent years however is one of guidance and direction. For example a compass can represent a change of direction in your life or a symbol to represent that your path will always stay true. There are many ways tis can be interoperated and you can add your own personal meaning too.

11. CROWS & RAVENS

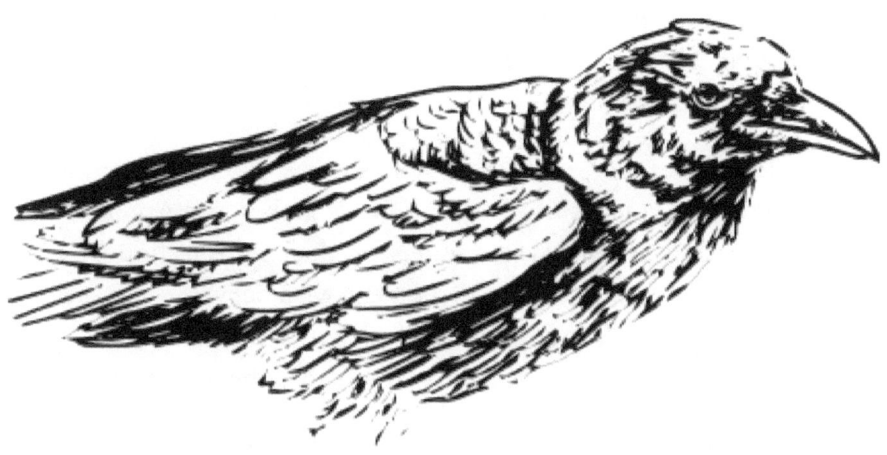

I'm going to lump crows and ravens together as crow tattoos are often applied with raven meaning and symbolism and pretty much no one knows the difference anyway!

Ravens have been referred to in the literature of most cultures throughout history at some point. Maybe it's because they're black, maybe it's because they make some pretty spooky sounds, maybe it's because they feed on dead animals or maybe it's all three making them a pretty potent symbol for some nasty stuff. Let's be honest, when most of us think of ravens we would probably associate them with a spooky old haunted castle or something similar.

There is a lot more to these animals however for example American Native Indians believed the Raven to be a trickster. In Chinese mythology a 3 legged raven is said to live in the sun and represent the dawn, daylight and dusk. In Japan the goddess Amaterasu is sometimes depicted as a giant Raven. Also in India, Brahma is also sometimes depicted as a Raven. The Aborigines thought the Raven got it's black coloration because it attempted to steal fire from seven sisters but failed and was charred black in the process. In Egypt the Raven symbolizes destruction and malevolence.

In Christian and Hebrew religious history Ravens were symbolic of impurity, deceit, and generally being unclean. Also in the Bible Noah cursed ravens for not returning to the ark with the news that flood was receding. Then again the Bible also says Ravens protected the prophets so it's not all bad.

That's a lot of meaning right? Well there's more! In Greek mythology the Raven is the messenger of the Sun Gods Helios and Apollo. Danes and Vikings used Raven banners on their ships to honor Odin seeing as Odin was said to have two ravens who delivered messages and gathered information for him to him. Which reinforces the Ravens most commonly associated symbolism of being a messenger.

Ravens are also considered to be very clever and are a symbol of knowledge. There is an old Scottish proverb that says "There is wisdom in a raven's head". Also "To have a raven's knowledge" is an old Irish proverb. In the Hebrides it was believed that giving your child its first drink from the skull of a Raven will give the them wisdom and powers of prophesy.

So there you have it, a bucket load of meaning and symbolism for the humble Raven! Obviously the main symbolism is as messenger but you now have a lot more meaning to choose from if you're thinking about getting a Raven tattoo so take your pick.

12. DAGGERS

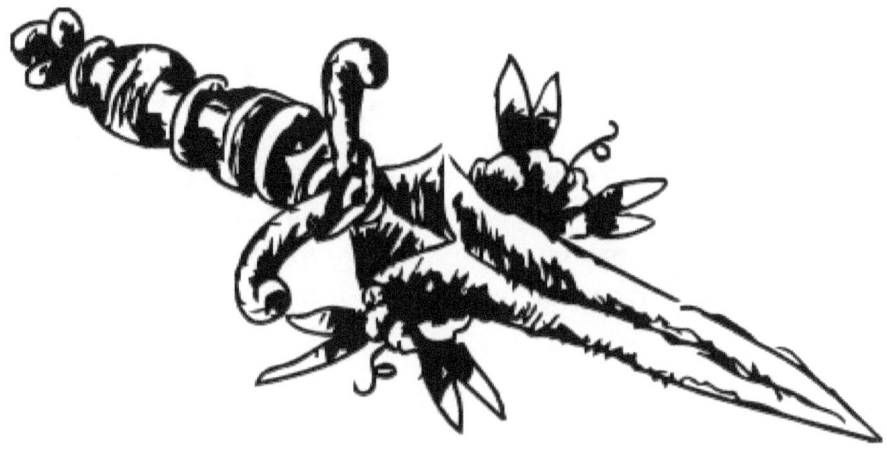

Daggers have been a popular tattoo design especially within the last 60 or so years. There is often not a lot of meaning attached to these tattoos and they are considered to be mainly decorative. However, there is a surprising amount of symbolism attached to the dagger.

Daggers are mainly representative of death, or more specifically, death caused by another person. It is also symbolic of ferocity and deadliness in general.

In the past a dagger dripping with blood was a message to others that the wearer had a concealed weapon and that they would use it if they had to. Due to this, a dripping dagger in modern times can be used to represent someone who is fearless and not willing to back down if confronted by someone who opposes them (not necessarily in a violent way although there are obvious connotations of violence attached with the dagger imagery).

A dagger and skull design can further illustrate the representation of death. A dagger through a heart can represent being betrayed by a boyfriend, girlfriend or spouse for example and serve as a reminder to not make the same mistakes again.

You may also see daggers in the teeth of skulls and some other designs. This theme was popularized in old pirate films when the pirates would board the enemy ship by swinging from a rope while holding their sword or dagger in their teeth. This type of design therefore represents readiness and ferocity.

The last common type of dagger design is a dagger going either into the skin or in and out again. This design is mainly used to symbolize being wounded by something or someone at some point in your life, which I'm sure everyone can relate to, and is therefore a popular tattoo design.

13. DICE

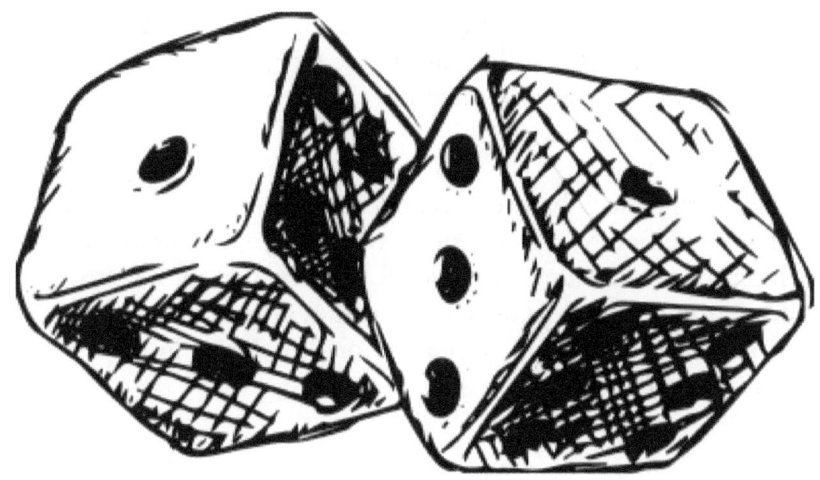

Dice have been a popular tattoo design for many years for various reasons and can hold many meanings.

Dice are first and foremost a symbol of luck. Dice games are all about getting lucky and throwing the number you want. This means that dice can be a great metaphor for life. From the moment we are born, some of us are born into a good family, some aren't. Some of us are born into poverty and some aren't. It's all luck, just like a dice game.

Also dice are a symbol of unpredictability. Just as we can't say what the next roll of the dice will be, we can't predict what life will throw at us no matter how hard we try.

Having a dice tattooed can show a belief that luck is important to you. After all, sometimes it can be more beneficial to just be lucky than to be talented and work hard for what you want.

The saying "The die are cast" is also relevant and can bring meaning to the dice tattoo. Attaching this kind of meaning to your tattoo can represent a decision you have made that there is no turning back on.

Dice are also commonly used imagery in gambling themed tattoos. In this instance the commonly lucky dice are often given a darker meaning. Many gambling tattoos are in reference to the dangers of gambling and the lifestyle that comes with it. A classic example of this is in the "Man's Ruin" designs. These designs feature many of the common weaknesses that men have such as drinking, gambling and women for example.

Most dice tattoos will feature two next to eachother. Something important to remember, that is often overlooked, is that he number shown on the upper side of the dice is of relevance to the tattoo. The number 7 is considered to be lucky and therefore is a common choice. Also, snake eyes is a popular choice as shown in the illustration in this book.

14. DOLPHINS

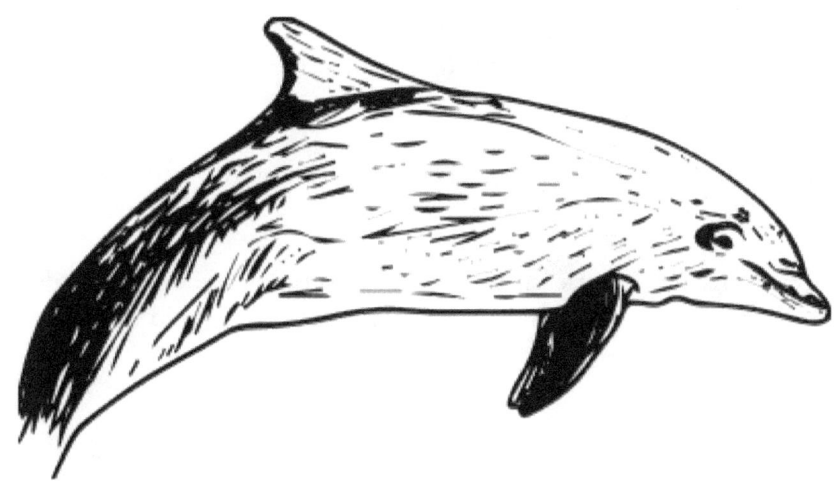

Unlike some other animals, the most common symbolism associated with dolphins comes from their behavior rather than their appearance.

Dolphins are considered to be very intelligent animals and therefor symbolize intelligence. They also symbolize playfulness and freedom.

Aside from the obvious meanings there is some stuff that you might not have considered. Right, time for a history lesson again I'm afraid. Sorry about that but it's needed in this case!

The Greeks and the Romans loved a good bit of mythology and they loved dolphins too. In a few of the myths there are accounts of dolphins bringing humans that were lost at sea safely back to shore. They were also messengers for Poseidon who was the Greek god of the oceans. So one possible meaning of a dolphin tattoo is to pay homage to or show your love for mythology. Weren't expecting that were you?

There's more, in Christianity dolphins are said to help transport the spirits of the faithful upon death. Also dolphins are considered a symbol of new life in Christianity so there's another unexpected meaning for you.

Similarly in Celtic culture the dolphin was also a symbol of new life due to the fact that they believed water could cleanse a person and bring a fresh lease of life. So a dolphin tattoo can certainly represent a new start or a change in your life.

Also, In Hinduism the Godess Ganga rode a dolphin and getting two dolphins together can represent Ying and Yang in a more artistic way.

Lastly, the native Americans believe that dolphins symbolize wisdom from within, so a dolphin tattoo can represent wisdom in this sense.

15. DOVES

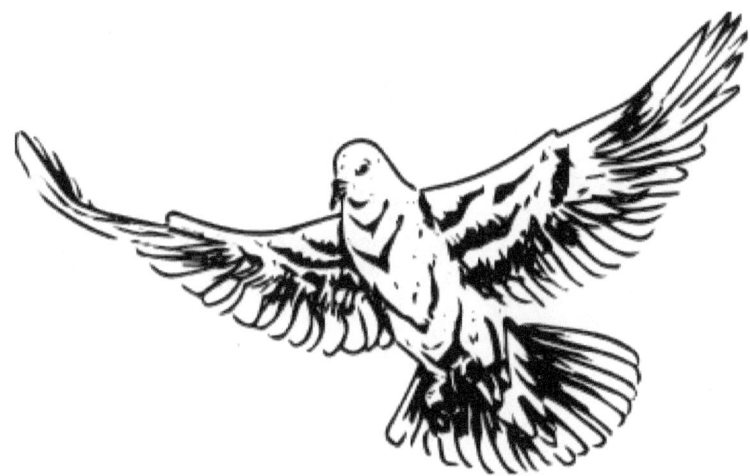

Doves are most often associated with love and peace. Also a very common piece of dove imagery is the dove with the olive branch in its mouth. If you weren't aware already, the reason behind the branch is because of the story of Noahs Ark were he releases a dove and it returns with a branch signaling the end of the flood. The early Christians in Rome used dove carrying an olive branch symbol as a symbol for peace.

Another little piece of a religious knowledge is that in Christian imagery the dove represents the holy spirit.

You may have also noticed that doves are often used as symbols for non-aggressive/pacifist events. Further emphasizing their symbolism for peace.

Interesting fact for you, you can milk a dove. Seriously...they produce milk. It lasts longer than any other type of milk too, because no bugger will drink it (Red Dwarf reference there). No but seriously they do produce milk for their young, which must be painful seeing as they are breast feeding something with a pointy beak (just a joke they don't have boobs really, that would just look weird. I think they feed it to them from their mouths) but that's beside the point. This makes them a symbol of motherhood, family and nurturing.

Now to the love bit, Aphrodite (or Venus if you're Roman) was often depicted as a curvy, beautiful woman with doves around her. It's here we have early recorded evidence of doves being associated with love.

There's not really much more to solidly associate them with love, but they are still widely a symbol of love. I suppose hanging out with the goddess of love is a good enough reason on its own but if that's not enough, they make pretty nice "cooing" noises and they're white so they look all pretty. So they just go nicely with love in general.

16. DRAGONS

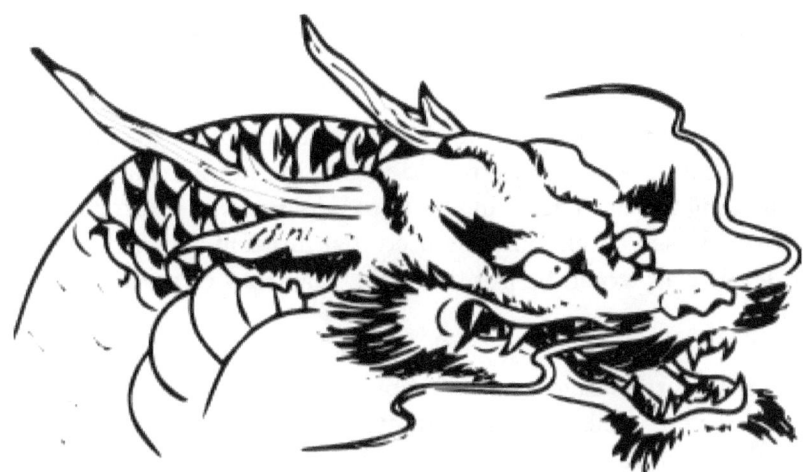

I'm going to mostly write this about the eastern style dragons because that's what 99% of people getting dragon tattoos get. But there is also standard kinda western dragons like you get in Game of Thrones or The Hobbit. These guys are typically evil, fire breathing badasses.

The western kind of dragons are mentioned in the bible twice one is called Leviathan and the other dragon, well, that's actually Satan. So yeah if you get a western style dragon then it's probably pretty evil according to history and religion.

However, the Easterners were much kinder to dragons and they ended up attaching all kinds of nice meanings to them.

In China dragons are creatures of legend and mythology. They are most commonly depicted with a serpent like scaled body and 4 legs. The dragon is a symbol of power, strength and good luck.

The dragon represents Yang and the Phoenix represents Yin. So get both and you've got some nice balance going on.

Traditionally Chinese dragons have power over water. This can be in the form of rivers, rain, floods etc. There as specific dragons for the seas around China and the villages near the water take this very seriously, building temples to worship the specific dragon king that they want to appease. This dragon king worship is still going on today, how many people actually believe dragons exist however is any ones guess.

Also another thing to note when getting the design of your dragon right which is almost always over looked is the number of fingers or toes the dragon has. The 5 fingered gold dragon was reserved for the Emperor himself. If anyone else used that motif in ancient China, their whole clan would be put to death. Yeah they took this stuff seriously.

The four fingered dragon was used by the fairly important people to show they were, well, fairly important. The 3 fingered dragon was something anyone could use. So now you know, lucky you have this book huh? Otherwise you might have got one with 5 fingers, traveled back in time, gone to ancient China and before you know it, they've cut your pony tail of and given you a ninja throwing star to the face.

17. DREAM CATCHERS

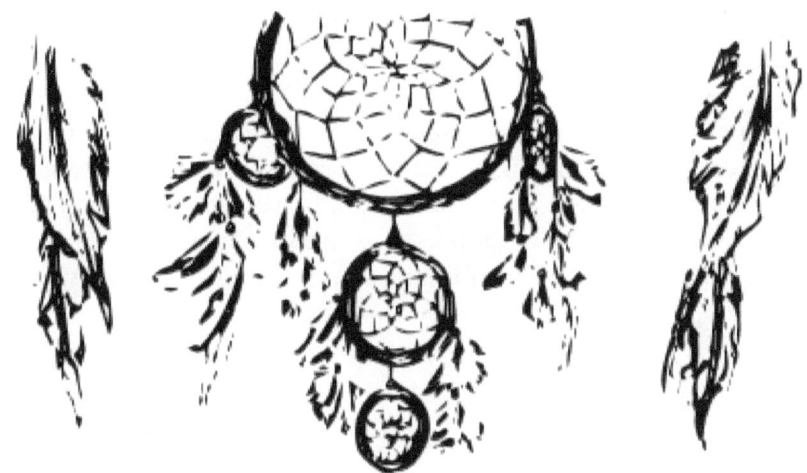

I think it's fairly obvious, but for those of you who didn't know, dream catchers are a Native American creation. Originally created by just one tribe, the dream catcher quickly spread throughout the Native American communities.

Due to this origin the dream catcher has become a symbol of unity among all of the Native American cultures. Having said this, there are some individuals that now believe the dream catcher has been commercialized to the point where they can no longer identify with it as a symbol of their culture.

The original tribe that created the dream catcher, The Oijbwe, said that there was a spider woman who took care of the children and the people on the land. When the Oijbwe spread across North America, she could no longer reach all of the people she needed to. So the women of the tribe made dream catchers to catch the children's negative thoughts during the night. Side note: traditionally the web was usually dyed red and the hoops could be either tear drop shaped or circular.

The most popular explanation for how the dream catcher is supposed to work is that the bad thoughts or dreams are caught and then disappear in daylight. It was also said that the good dreams would be caught and pass down the feathers to the person sleeping below. The other way some people say they work is that they let the bad thoughts pass through and catch the good thoughts and again, pass them down to the person sleeping below. Either way, it's all good stuff.

Something that makes dream catchers a good tattoo design is the fact that the web areas in the center have no set structure. This enables you to add hidden meaning to the design. For example you can add a certain number of strings to represent a number such as an age or something more obscure like the house number of the house you grew up in.

18. EAGLES

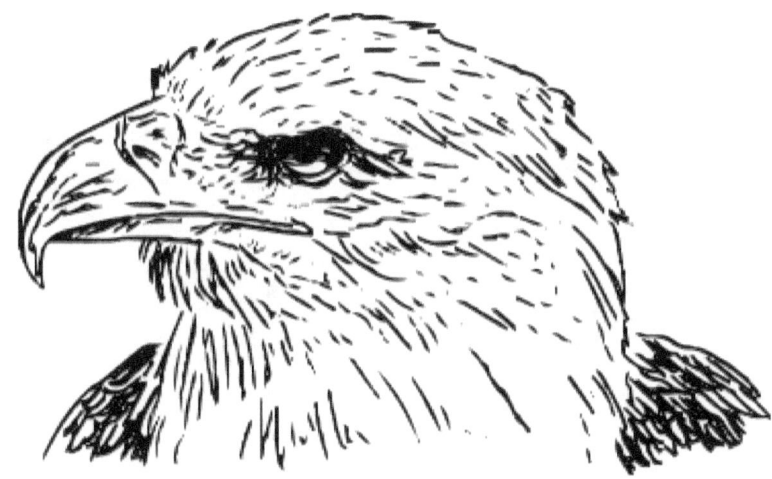

Eagles have been a very popular symbol in many countries and cultures throughout history and have a huge amount of meaning attached to them.

When I think of Eagles being used as a symbol in a historical sense the first thing that springs to mind is the Roman Empire, they loved a good eagle and used them as a symbol of power and strength. The Romans also connected eagles with Jupiter (the God not the planet), while the Greeks associated the eagle with Zeus. The Germanic tribes connected eagles with Odin. So that's some pretty respectable friends the eagle has there.

I was once walking round a falconry/zoo kind of place and walked round a corner just looking at the owls and there in front of me was an eagle. It was MASSIVE! It actually shocked me just seeing the sheer size and wingspan of this thing, then it started making weird, scary eagle noises and I was thinking, I would not mess with this dude! So I can see why they are such a powerful symbol of strength.

This is probably why so many nations and cultures such as The Spanish Empire, The Byzantine Empire, The Holy Roman Empire, The Russian Empire and The German Empire have all chosen to use the eagle crest.

Of course the bald eagle is widely associated with the United States of America in modern times due to the use of the eagle in the Great Seal and also due to the fact that the bald eagle is native to the continent.

So the main symbolism of the eagle is power and strength. As with all birds the eagle also represents freedom.

19. FEATHERS

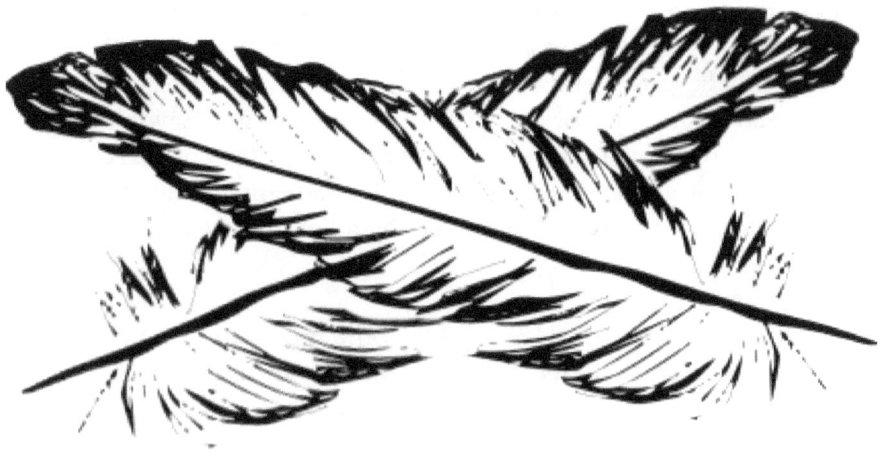

I know from my years of tattooing that feathers are pretty damn popular! Especially with girls, although I have tattooed them on guys too. They do make great tattoo designs and they can be tattooed in a huge range of styles and are just a nice looking design in general. It's pretty hard to go wrong with a feather.

The most common meaning given to feathers is due to the fact that they come from birds and bird are a symbol is freedom due to their ability to fly freely wherever they want. However there is a lot more to them that this if you're looking for alternative or a deeper meaning.

The instances of feather symbolism throughout history generally refer to some sort of spiritual ascension. Native Americans wore feathers to symbolize their connection to the spirit world and show their wisdom. Also in Native American culture feathers were representative of the thunder gods and the wind and the air.

In Celtic culture the Druids would also wear feathers, this time in the form of feather robes. They believed that by wearing the feathers they could ascend to a spiritual world in the presence of the sky gods. So more sky related god stuff just like the Native Americans.

Yet again, more sky gods for the Egyptians who used feathers to represent the sky gods too. Bit weirder though this time. Ma'at, who was the Egyptian goddess of justice, would take the heart of someone who just kicked the bucket and weigh it against the weight of a feather. She did this to judge their soul. Bit of an unfair test if you ask me but maybe gravity works differently in the ancient Egyptian afterlife? More likely it's a metaphor for having a "heavy heart", which I think is some great symbolism. Get a feather/heart tattoo and you have a nice metaphor for having a light hearted, carefree outlook on life.

The Christian symbolism is pretty awesome too. Three feathers together symbolizes charity, hope and faith. They used to use this symbol on signets rings which they pressed into wax to seal their letters. If you got a letter from someone with the three feather symbol it was supposed to mean that the writer of the letter is a virtuous person.

20. HEARTS

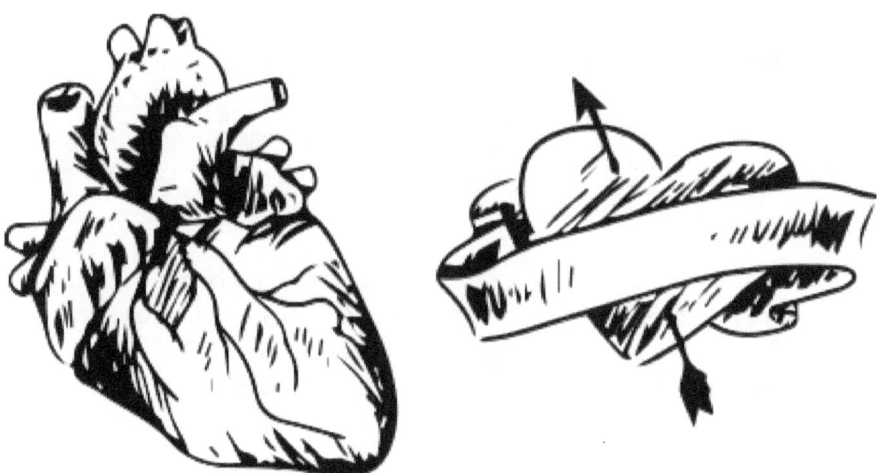

Well I think it's fairly obvious that the love heart symbol represents love as the name would suggest. Right, next chapter.

I am of course joking and there is more to heart tattoos than meets the eye. You've got your love hearts, hearts and banners, arrow hearts, broken hearts, anatomically correct hearts, sacred hearts and more.

Hearts generally symbolize romantic love but not exclusively, the "mom heart" was popularized around about the 1950's when electric tattooing really gained some decent momentum and sailors were off, far from home, missing their family and not sure if they were even going to go home or get shot first. This design is one of the all-time most iconic tattoo designs and deserves massive props.

Obviously you could get a different name in the banner as many people do and the tattoo can apply to anyone. Although speaking from experience, the amount of people who get cover-ups after getting something like that with their girlfriends name that they met a few months ago leads me to believe the getting "Mom" is a much more sensible option.

Arrow hearts are another popular one because of everyone's favorite little love cherub, Cupid, and his arrows. Arrow hearts are definitely 100% romantic so don't get one of those for your mum.

Broken hearts and dagger hearts are used to represent having had bad luck in love. A broken heart usually means just that, your heart has been broken in the past. A dagger through the heart means pretty much the same thing but also that you were betrayed in the process of having your heart broken.

Anatomically correct hearts are pretty gory let's be honest but they are a more intricate artistic way of depicting heart symbolism. So you could still go for a banner saying mom with an anatomical heart, same goes for arrows, daggers and everything else really. Up to personal preference!

The last type of heart I want to cover is The Sacred Heart, also known as "The Most Sacred Heart of Jesus". It's a Roman Catholic devotion and is very widely practiced among the members of this religion. It's a symbol for taking Christ's physical heart as the representation of his divine love for humanity.

21. KEYS & PADLOCKS

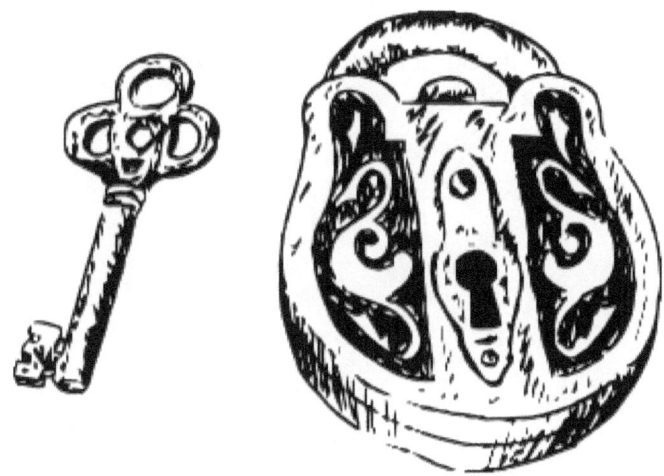

Due to the intricate vintage motifs that can be incorporated to the designs, key and padlock tattoos have become very popular in recent years.

The most common meaning given to these types of tattoos is along the lines of the "key to my heart" theme. Due to this, some couples will get a matching key tattoo to show they have the key to each other's hearts. There are variations of this such as the woman having a heart shaped padlock and the man getting the key etc. When the "key to my heart" meaning is used, the padlock is often heart shaped.

One overlooked piece of symbolism for key tattoos, that I thought of myself may I add, is that keys symbolize responsibility. The reason I say this is because I noticed one day how many keys I had. I mad one for my flat, some for the tattoo studio etc. I realized that the more keys I had, the more responsibility I had. So I think that's a pretty good one!

Padlocks have been associated with romantic notions throughout history, probably due to their links with permanence and security. For a long time heart shaped lockets have been worn with a lock of their partners hair enclosed inside for example.

Both key and padlock tattoos are symbolic of either unlocking something or locking it away. This makes them extremely versatile and easy to attach a more personal meaning to. For example they can represent a secret that you have lock away and left behind or unlocking a new chapter in your life.

22. KOI

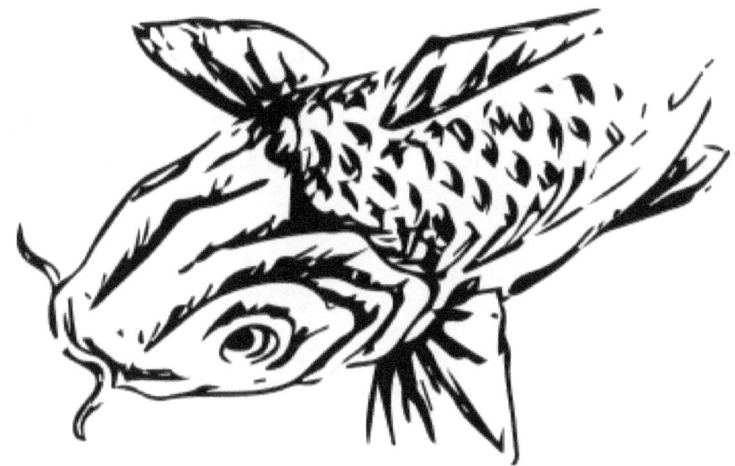

Koi tattoos originated in the far east and are most often tattooed in a Japanese style and commonly worked into sleeve designs. However, koi can also be smaller individual tattoos and tattooed in a variety of styles.

In Japanese legend koi can jump up the yellow river and become dragons. Due to this, koi are often associated with personal improvement and reaching your goals. Koi with dragon heads, imaginatively named "Dragon Koi", are a popular design is Japanese artwork due to this piece of mythology and also make a great variation on the typical koi tattoo design.

Koi are also symbols of good luck and good fortune. There are a lot of variations such as colour and direction that dictate the meaning of the koi tattoo. This is pretty much always overlooked and people just get whatever colour they think looks good.

Red koi are symbolic of love. Red is traditionally considered to be a strong and masculine colour though so may not be the best choice for women.

Black koi are representative of overcoming particularly difficult or painful struggles and challenges in your life. In this way they are also associated with success.

A blue koi swimming upwards can be symbolic of a challenge or problem that you are facing. If a blue koi is swimming downwards it is more likely to represent a challenge that is in your past. Blue koi, as with red koi, are considered to be masculine. They don't leave many colours for the ladies do they? Oh, they can also represent reproduction.

23. KRAKEN

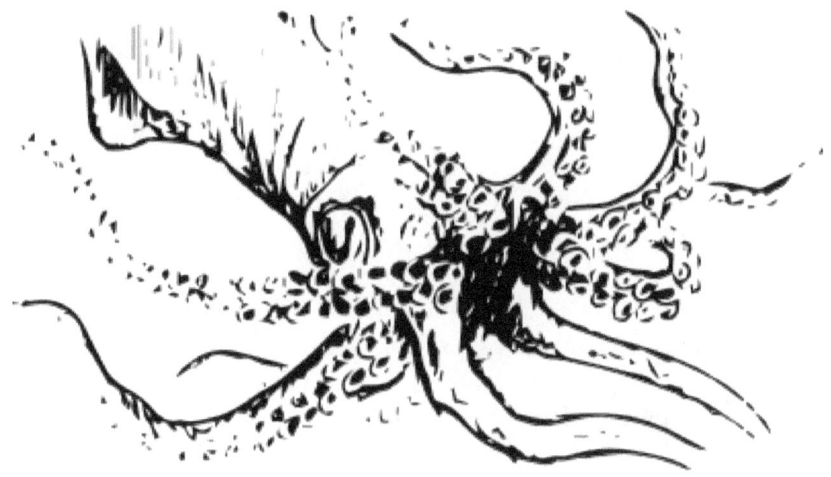

Kraken have been mentioned as early as the 12th century in Norway but in the 18th century paintings and illustrations of these mythical creatures have cropped up.

Kraken are most commonly depicted as a huge octopus or squid like creature. Personally I like the giant squid look better, hence why I drew the squid above and not the octopus style one. It's up to personal preference though.

There are some variations of the kraken that aren't what we are typically used to seeing however. Some of them had spikes on their tentacles, but in the earliest descriptions of the kraken they were said to be more crab like than anything else and were so large they were often mistaken for islands.

The modern octopus or squid style Kraken however, what we see in artworks and tattoos designs are almost always in the process of attacking a ship. This would probably be due to sailors stories of being attacked by the Kraken and living to tell the tale.

The question is, were these sailors just trying to act cool in front of their mates and say they survived a Kraken attack, or was there something more to the tales than meets the eye?

The sailors telling these stories may have actually seen a giant squid. A creature that we still know all too little about. It has been said that they are large enough to take on a whale and in the 1930's there are a accounts of a giant squid attacking a ship. Now, these squid didn't come off too well seeing as they inevitably got caught in the ships propellers and promptly sliced up, but it does show they are willing to attack ships, probably as they were mistakenly thinking they were attacking a whale.

So the stories of old may well have some truth to them. I mean who's to say that hundreds of years ago there wasn't giant squid that grew even larger than the few we have seen, that did in fact manage to break a few ships wooden hulls or capsize them and send the unfortunate sailors to their watery graves? Some of the ships back then were pretty small so I think it seems like a realistic theory.

As for meaning and symbolism, other than death and destruction there isn't a lot there! I don't think it matters though seeing as their story is good enough on its own.

24. LIONS

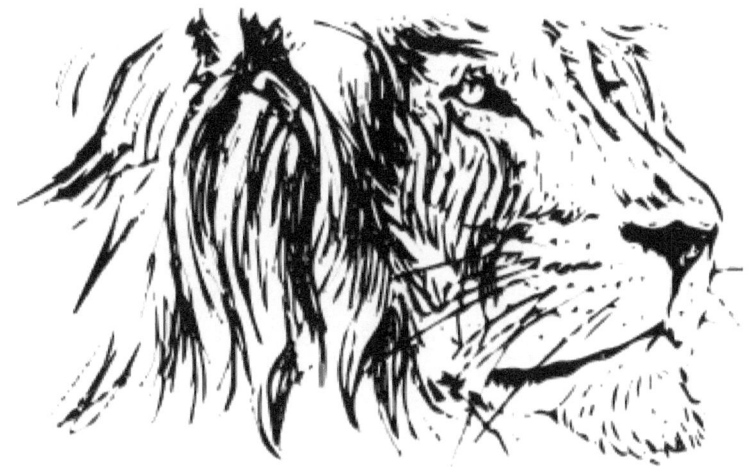

Right, first things first, Lions are obviously the Zodiac symbol for Leo's which is probably why at least 50% of people get them. So that's that one out of the way! There a lot more meaning behind lions and they can be a great choice of tattoo for anyone.

Lions are commonly associated with strength and power and are commonly seen as a kingly animal. Therefore lion tattoos can represent personal strength whether it be physical or mental etc.

Due to the way in which lion prides work, with one alpha male watching over the rest of the pride, the lion can be a symbol of family and protection over that family.

Also, for the same reasons, the lion can also be used to represent authority and natural leadership qualities.

Going back to the Zodiac deal, I should probably mention that Leo is a sun sign and the Lion is associated with the sun. The link is not only due to star signs but also because of the golden fur and the lions mane being kind of similar to the rays around the sun. In an astrological/Zodiac sense the lion represents Passion, Generosity, Loyalty, Influence, Leadership and Determination.

Lions can also be representative of wisdom due to their proud, noble demeanor. So there's a whole lot of meaning and symbolism there that covers pretty much all bases!

25. LIZARDS

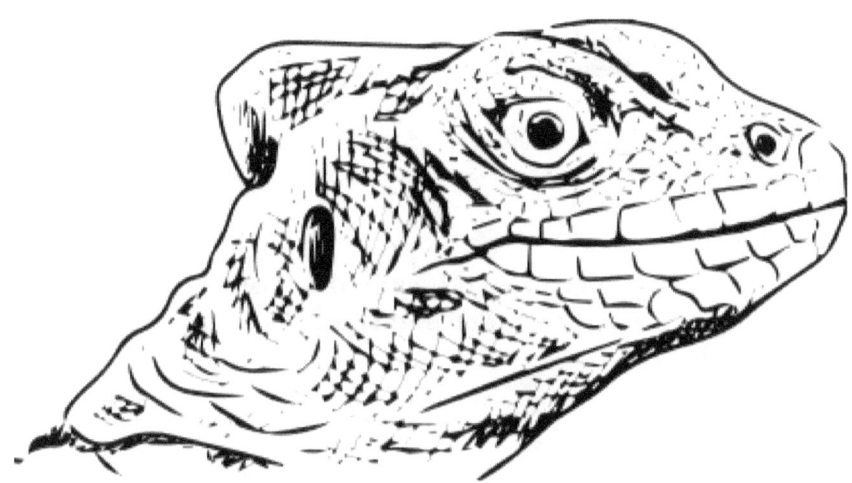

Lizards are pretty amazing creatures. They come in all shapes and sizes and are probably one of the most versatile species of animal going. To top it off, they're also very popular as tattoo designs!

The Greeks and Egyptians associated the lizards good fortune and wisdom. In fact, the Egyptian hieroglyphic symbol for abundance and wealth very closely resembles a lizard.

In some regions of Africa, lizards are carved in the walls of houses to bring peace to the home and ward of any evil spirits that might be lurking about. That's right, African malevolent spirits are scared of lizards apparently.

You may have heard of the phrase "lizard brain", it's not the most common one so you might not have but, it is a thing trust me. To have a lizard brain means to be in touch with your instincts and be more of a survivalist than others. People with a lizard brain will also follow their gut feelings and their primal urges more than other people.

Due to the vast variety of lizards found all over the world, a lizard tattoo can represent versatility and adaptability to different situations and circumstances.

Other notable mentions in the lizard category go to these chaps:

Salamander tattoos represent a passionate person who is able to come through troublesome situations without being harmed.

Gecko tattoos can represent regeneration due to their ability to grow back lost body parts. They're also expert climbers linking them strongly with agility.

Last but not least, our crazy eyed friends, the Chameleon. These guys represent illusion and secrecy due to their excellent ability to camouflage themselves.

26. LOTUS FLOWERS

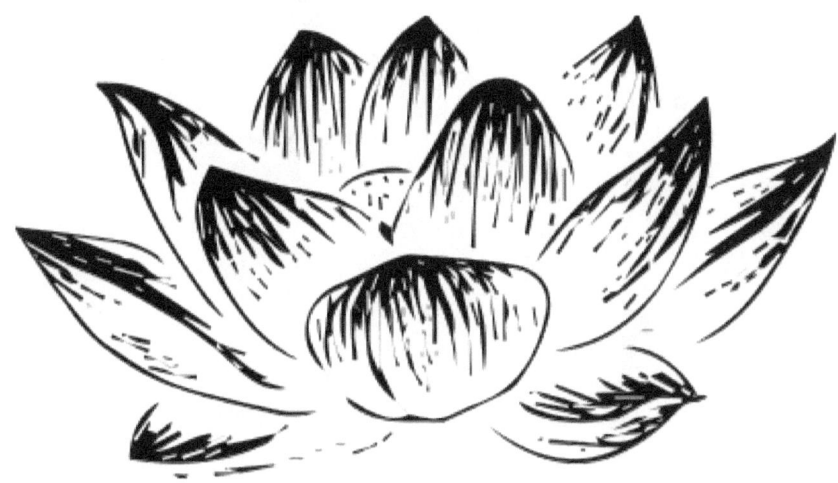

Lotus flowers are renowned for being extremely beautiful flowers that grow out of murky or dirty ponds. Due to this the lotus flower has become heavily associated with beauty and purity, particularly in eastern countries.

The lotus flower holds a great deal of significance is Buddhism. The Buddhists also associate with flower with purity but also spiritual awakening and faithfulness.

There are different colours of lotus flower that all hold different meanings.

A blue lotus represents the spirit winning over the mind or knowledge. A white lotus represents a spiritual awakening and the calming of your nature. Purple lotus flowers are often depicted in a more symmetrical design with eight petals. This represents the noble eightfold path which is one of the principal teachings of the Buddha which is said to lead to spiritual awakening. The pink lotus is considered to be the supreme lotus as seen as the true lotus of Buddha. A Red lotus is representative of the heart and love.

The lotus flower also holds a great deal of meaning and significance in Hinduism. In Hinduism the lotus is usually white and is symbolic of beauty, fertility, prosperity, spirituality, and eternity. The lotus flower appears in many depictions of the Hindu gods and goddesses.

One last thing to mention is that a partially open lotus flower us symbolic of a person who hasn't, but has the ability and potential to, unfold and develop into who they will one day become.

27. MAGPIES

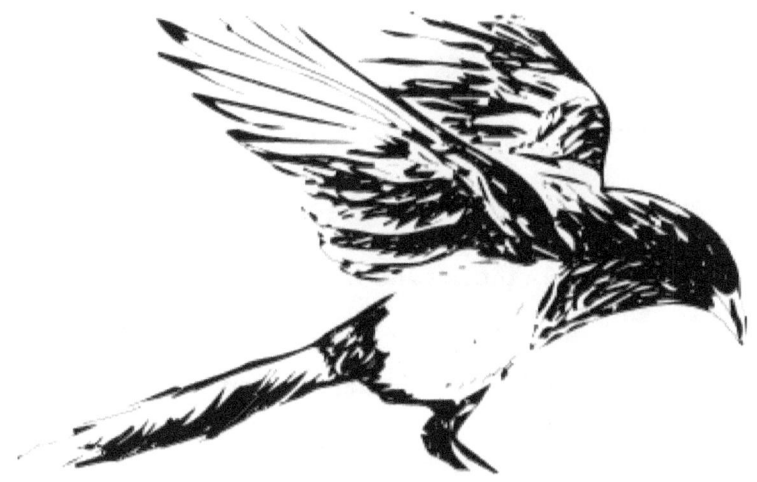

Now I ain't saying she a gold digga, but…ok that bloody magpie just stole my wedding ring…and the tin foil I had my sandwich wrapped in!

So I think we all know that magpies are generally associated with liking shiny things and taking them to put in their super pimped out blingtastic nest (they actually do steal shiny things, that's not a myth). But is there more to this winged thief than meets the eye?

Well for starters, did you know that the common Magpie mates for life? This means they can be associated with family, devotion, loyalty and love.

In China the magpie is a symbol of good fortune and happiness. Killing one is a bit like breaking a mirror over here, it brings you bad luck. The Manchu people in China even regard Magpies as a sacred bird and under the Manchu dynasty the Magpie was a symbol of imperial rule. So if you're incorporating one into an eastern themed sleeve or something you might want to keep that in mind.

In Chinese and Korean legend the Magpie Bridge joins 3 stars of Aquila (called the Cowherd) to Lyra, (called the Spinning Damsel) across the river that is the Milky Way on the 7th night of the 7th moon. Don't ask me exactly what that means because, to be honest, I don't have a clue but it sounds pretty cool.

Koreans also considered magpies to be messengers that brought good news where as in Mongolia thought that the Magpie was a very intelligent bird with the ability to control the weather.

The Germans said that one magpie alone was unlucky, two indicated happiness or marriage, three means a successful journey, four means that you will receive good news and five means that you will have someone coming to visit you.

The Greeks seemed to have a meaning for everything didn't they? The Magpie is no exception. They considered the magpie a bit of a drunkard I'm afraid as it was scared to Bacchus the God of wine. Therefore the magpie became associated with being a wee bit merry.

Us English people see a lone magpie as a symbol of bad luck as with many predominantly Christian regions. This is probably due to the fact that magpies were the only bird that refused to enter the ark. In Somerset, not too far from me, some people used to carry an onion on them at all times to provide protection against magpies as they were also thought to be an omen of death.

In reference to magpies my nan always said: One for sorrow, two for joy, three for a girl, four for a boy, five for silver, six for gold and seven for a secret never to be told. Apparently that's a pretty popular saying so there's some more meaning for you.

28. MOTHS

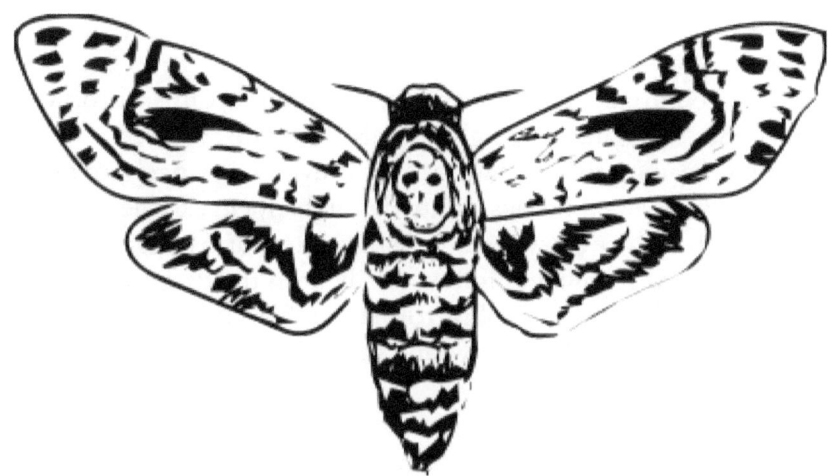

The most common type of moth tattoo is the Death's-Head Hawkmoth as shown above. Obviously there are a multitude of other moths to choose from in a variety of shapes, colours and sizes so there's no need to limit yourself. But as I said, this is by far the most commonly used moth for tattoo designs.

Because of the Death's-Head's skull like marking and the high pitched squeaking sound it makes it has been associated with the occult and put into the same kind of category as bats, ravens, black cats and rats.

Moses Harris, an entomologist, wrote this lovely little quote about these moths in 1840, "It is regarded not as the creation of a benevolent being, but the device of evil spirits—spirits enemies to man—conceived and fabricated in the dark, and the very shining of its eyes is thought to represent the fiery element whence it is supposed to have proceeded. Flying into their apartments in the evening at times it extinguishes the light; foretelling war, pestilence, hunger, death to man and beast".

Sounds like something out of Lord of the Rings! It up to you whether you think that awesome or creepy and weird. As I said though if you're not into that kind of thing there's plenty of other moths out there for you to choose from with a lot of meaning and symbolism attached due to the many interesting characteristics of these creatures.

Moths are nocturnal and can therefore represent dreams, shadows. The way they navigate using light can also provide some very interesting meaning to your tattoo. Moths evolved to navigate by moon light (unproven but it's pretty damn likely) back when we hadn't put up lights everywhere to distract them and buggered everything up. Moths would follow this light in the darkness and not stop. This is a fantastic metaphor for having faith in something and following that faith without wavering through the darkness.

This meaning can also be flipped on its head. Moths can be used to represent the meaning that sometimes blind faith can lead to destruction. This is due to the fact that moths are so sure that following light is the right way to go that they will fly straight into fire and obviously perish pretty quickly. Then again that could represent sacrifice for the sake of keeping faith in something. Depends on how you want to look at it!

One final thing to point out is that moths can blend in with their surroundings such as leaves, trees and branches to the point where they are practically invisible, even during broad daylight. This can hold meaning for people who maybe feel like they have a side to their personality that makes them need to hide from time to time or for someone who blends in at first sight but is much more when seen for who they really are.

29. OWLS

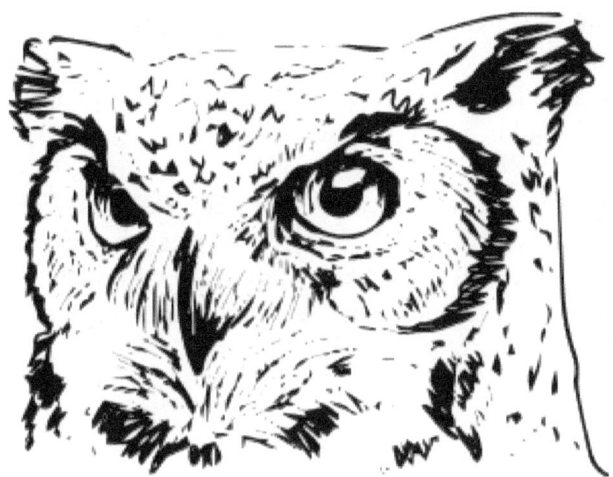

Ah the owl, a hugely popular tattoo design in recent times being mainly favored by old school and neo-traditional enthusiasts but also tattooed in pretty much any style imaginable!

I think the first thing to mention about the meaning behind owl tattoos is the obvious one that everyone thinks of, wisdom. Owls are constantly seen as being these wise old birds that sit there on a branch looking like they know it all. Owls are in fact pretty damn stupid.

The reason they are seen as being smart may well be something to do with the fact that they look like they should be intelligent but there's a bit more to it than that. The earliest evidence of the owls connection with being a brain box is found way back in ancient Greece. Owls were strongly associated with Athena who was the Greek goddess of wisdom and foresight. So yes the owl does definitely represent wisdom although in actual fact they are pretty stupid and the foresight bit leads me nicely onto my next point.

Owls have got a seriously good set of peepers on them. This makes them a symbol of perception, and of course, foresight. This is further enforced by the fact that the owl can turn its head 270 degrees making it pretty hard to sneak anything past an owl.

Now obviously owls are nocturnal and they do make that creepy owl sound at night. In ancient cultures, anything that came out at night was pretty much considered to be a bit of a git. So the owl was portrayed somewhat of a poor light in the past but not to the point of bats for example. Also no one really even thinks about that anymore so I wouldn't worry about that one.

As they do well in the dark however they can be considered another symbol of doing well during dark times in your life. This time however the owl would more likely symbolize you make it through using foresight and knowledge rather than something like faith or strength for example.

30. PANTHERS

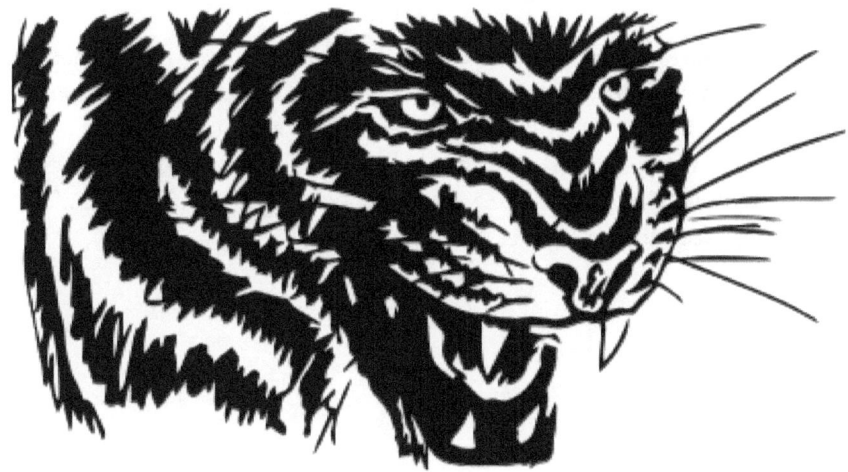

An all-time classic, the crawling panther tattoo has been a staple of all tattoo studios for a long time. These days, the neo-traditional panther head seems to be more of a popular choice. Whatever style you choose the panther has a great deal of symbolism and a solid place in tattoo history and culture.

Little fact for you before we get started on this one, a panther isn't actually a species of big cat in its own right. A panther is just a big cat such as a jaguar or a leopard with black pigmentation.

As for the ancient history aspect, there's a fair bit going on. The Greeks used the panther as a symbol for Dionysus, the god of wine theatre and ecstasy. Therefore the panther was a symbol of freeing yourself and liberation.

The Pagans saw the panther as a symbol of female power and motherhood, very similar to Chinese symbolism where they also see the panther as a symbol of motherhood.

Amund Dietzel is widely accredited with being the first to use the crawling panther design in tattooing after discovering an illustration of it in a book called Minute Myths by Marie Schubert. If you wanted to pay homage to the first ever panther design and go as traditional as possible you could look it up and get that exact design and have a great story to tell!

As I mentioned panthers are known for being great mothers, they are also known with fiercely defending their cubs fiercely. This makes them a great tattoo to symbolize protection over your family.

Obviously panthers symbolize power and strength but they are also symbolic of freedom, mystery and stealth.

31. PHOENIX

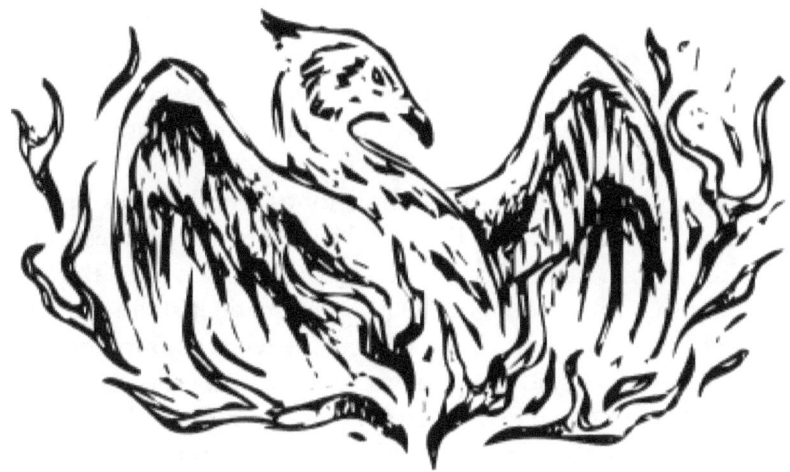

The Phoenix is the last of the three mythical animals that are commonly tattooed (the other being dragons and kraken). The Phoenix is often tattooed in a Japanese style as part of sleeves or back pieces but can be done in a number of different styles.

To get to the root of where the myth of the phoenix started and where we get our modern imagery of the phoenix, we need to once again head back to the history books.

In Greek mythology the phoenix is a bird that is reborn every time it dies, rising fresh from its own ashes. The Greeks heavily linked the phoenix with the sun. Early Christians took on the symbol and probably came up with the story of the phoenix dying by fire although there are other versions where it just dies and decomposes before being reborn. Some stories said the phoenix lived for over 1400 years.

History also tells us that the phoenix "could symbolize renewal in general as well as the sun, time, the empire, metempsychosis, consecration, resurrection, life in the heavenly Paradise, Christ, Mary, virginity, the exceptional man, and certain aspects of Christian life".

So who invented the phoenix? It's thought that it was probably the

Egyptians but there's similarities between the Greek and the Egyptian phoenix so it could be a bit of a mix between them.

In medieval times the phoenix was painted and illustrated in literature. They often gave the phoenix a nimbus (halo like glow around the head) to represent the phoenix's connection with the sun, sometimes with 7 rays, like Helios (the sun in Greek mythology).

Just a warning I'm going to say a whole lot of weird names here, just go with it. As for appearance Pliny said that they have a crest on top of their head while Ezekiel compared the phoenix to a rooster. Tacitus said that the colours of the phoenix made it stand out from any other bird although he didn't say exactly what colours they were. Herodotus, however said the phoenix was red and yellow and Ezekiel kind of confirmed this when he said the phoenix has red legs and yellow eyes. It was all going well until Lactantius comes along as says sapphire blue eyes and yellow-gold scales legs with rose-colored talons. Then R. Van den Broek, Herodotus, Pliny, Solinus, and Philostratus describe the phoenix as being pretty much the same size as an eagle. Then Lactantius and Ezekiel start saying that they're bigger than ostriches. So I guess you're going to have to make your own mind up!

But yeah, in general, the main meaning for these mythical birds is obviously re-birth. This meaning is great for people who have reinvented themselves and started fresh.

32. PIN-UP GIRLS

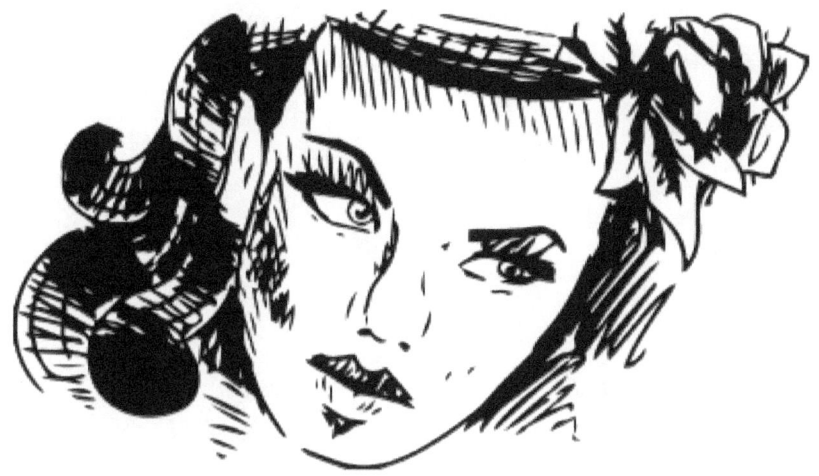

Pin-up girls were models who had their photos printed and distributed with the intention of, you guessed it, people pinning up their photos on the wall.

These photos, or artworks of the pin-up models were extremely popular throughout the world and especially amongst soldiers in both the first and second World Wars on both sides. During the war, to help keep up moral, free copies of magazines were shipped out to soldiers featuring the models wearing army and navy uniforms.

Unsurprisingly, as these girls were such an inspiration to the fighting men, some of them would choose to get the images of these women permanently tattooed. This is where the pin-up tattoo design would have originated.

Of course you didn't have to be in the military to get a pin-up tattoo and a lot of men, and sometimes women, who weren't in the forces would also get these tattoos.

Pin-up tattoos are still very popular to this day with more and more women joining in on the craze and getting the tattoo to represent femininity and empowerment.

The meaning for men is usually a lot more superficial to say the least! But I don't see a problem with that personally. I would also see it as being a sign of respect to those soldiers who saw the pin-up girls as a symbol of home and of hope.

33. ROSES

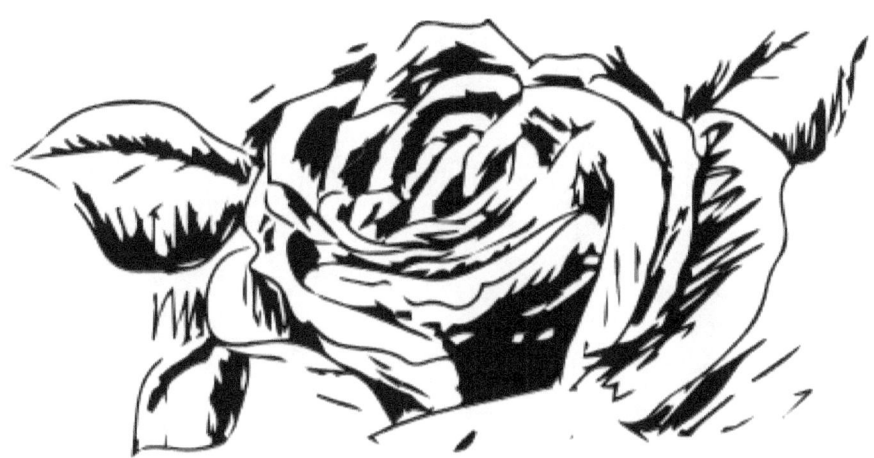

I would go far as to say that roses are probably the most tattooed design ever in all its various shapes and forms. Don't quote me on that but roses are tattoo designs in their own right, then they are also used to border other designs and to fill gaps in sleeves. What is used more than roses?

Roses are symbols of love. The rose was used along with the heart symbol right at the start of modern tattoo as the two primary tattoos to symbolize love and the humble rose tattoo has gone from strength to strength ever since.

The earliest recorded instance of roses being associated with love that I found was, as ever, the Greeks. They heavily associated roses with both Aphrodite and Venus, goddesses of love.

So obviously roses, and in particular the red rose, symbolize love. But what do the other colours of rose mean?

White roses symbolize innocence and humility. Yellow roses represent friendship and joy. Pink surprisingly represents gratitude, admiration and appreciation. Orange roses symbolize enthusiasm and desire. Both lilac and purple colour roses represent infatuation and love at first sight.

You may also want to give some thought to the number of petals on the rose or the number of roses as these numbers can be used to represent some kind of hidden meaning for you.

34. SCORPIONS

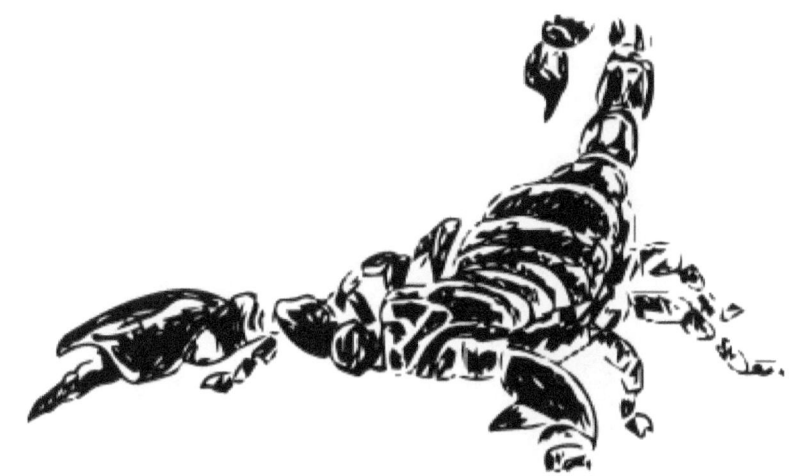

Scorpions are most commonly associated with self-defense mainly because of their formidable stance when they feel threatened. Pincers at the ready, tail poised with sting at the ready and their armored plates all show off their ability to defend themselves against anything that way want to cause them harm.

Scorpions are also obviously one of the signs of the zodiac so if that's your reason for getting it then you already know why so no point in me covering that!

Scorpions have also been associated with life and death throughout history. The Egyptians believed that scorpions were servants of Selket who was the guardian that protected souls on their way to the afterlife.

Now, scorpion stings don't always have the same effect. In African lore, scorpion stings could actually have healing properties... apparently. They did also know that they could kill you though. Scorpion stings can be hallucinogenic and the shamans found this out and used the venom to assist in their spiritual journeys.

Due to the fact that scorpions live in pretty harsh environments, they can be seen as symbols of triumphing over difficulties in your life.

The last thing to mention is that scorpions are commonly associated with the sun. This means that the scorpion symbolizes some sun like qualities like energy, vitality and Radiance.

35. SHARKS

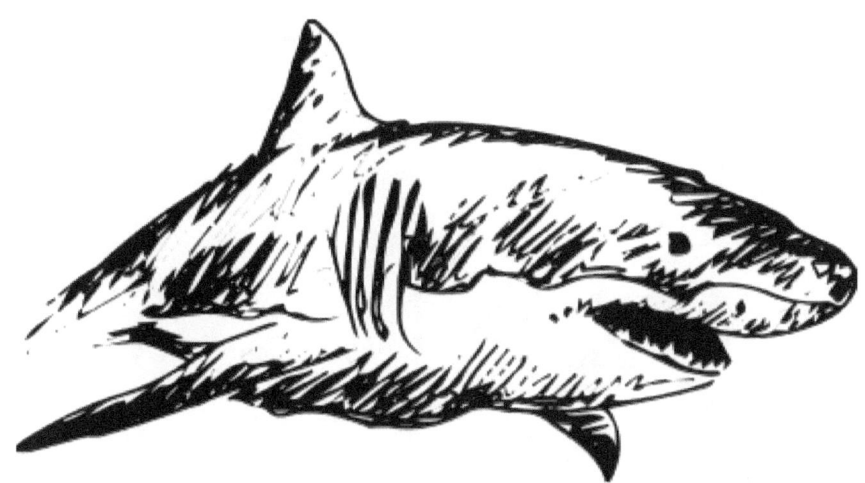

The shark has some obvious connotations such as fear and aggression, but there is a lot more to the symbolism and meaning associated with sharks than just being a bad ass killing machine.

The Maori regard the shark as "king of the waters". It's a fairly accurate description I suppose! In their culture the shark is a potent symbol of victory and power.

For sailors, many servicemen, pirates and pretty much anyone else who spends a good amount of time at sea may well consider the shark tattoo a symbol of protection while on the water. Much like a good luck charm or how the ancient Celts regarded their rune tattoos as protection in battle.

Sharks were a popular tattoo for the men of the navy. While traveling from port to port the navy men would get tattoos at the ports, where the tattoo studios inevitably were because they weren't stupid, to remind them of their travels. Obviously as they were in the navy a shark would have been a popular choice.

There are many traits that a shark symbolizes. As mentioned they certainly represent power, to be more precise a raw primal power. They also certainly represent natural instinct and focus.

Sharks also seem to be fearless and not show any emotion or hesitation they do what needs to be done. I would say these traits are also representative of confidence and self-assurance.

So there's a lot more meaning there than what most people automatically think of. This makes sharks a great tattoo idea if you're a fan of hidden meaning in your tattoos.

36. SHIPS

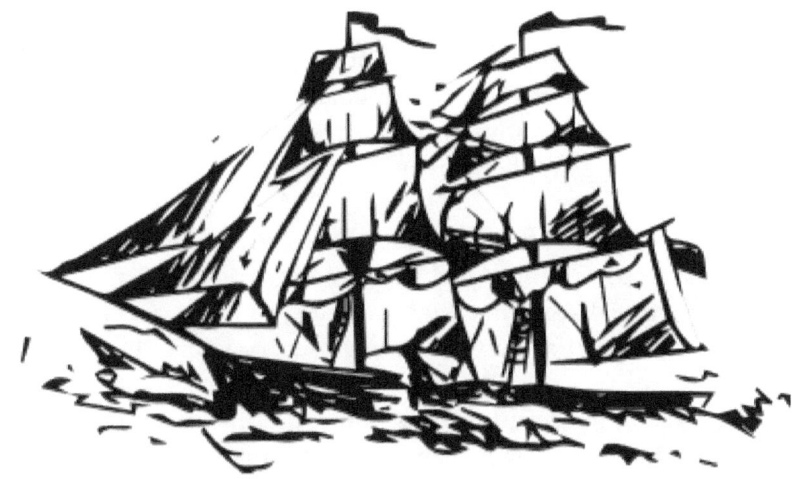

Now obviously there's a lot of types of ship. Surprisingly enough though I'm not going to massively concern myself with the meaning behind oil liners and tug boats. I will be mainly focusing on the "tall ship" or "ship of the line" style tattoos.

If you haven't heard those names before then a tall ship just means a ship with tall masts and sails. A ship of the line is so called because when tall ships went into battle back in the days of canons and "full broad sides", all of the ships in the fleet would typically sail in a line together so... ships of the line.

Ship tattoos are obviously another naval tattoo that would have been popular among sailors in the navy and any other sea fairing types in general really.

One thing a ship tattoo can symbolize is adventure. Ships are a symbol of sailing into the unknown and embarking on an adventure. So if you're maybe going traveling or taking on a new challenge a ship tattoo would be an excellent way to remember it.

However ship tattoos can also represent home. Sailors would often talk about going home as back in the day, a ship full of sweaty blokes and begin shot at with canons couldn't have been the idea place to be. At that point their mums cooking probably seemed like paradise to them.

Many of the men sailing these ships knew that once they set foot on that ship there was a higher than slim chance that they may never return home. In this way ship tattoos can symbolize bravery and honor or a sense of duty that drives you on.

Ships are also symbols of navigation and direction. This means they can be a great tattoo to make a change in direction in your life. Or maybe you have realized what path you need to be on and the ship tattoo can mark the new course you have set for yourself.

Lastly, these old ships could well last a few lifetimes and bear many scars of war. Due to this, ships can be a great metaphor for having a troubled past and maybe bearing the scars but, you carried on and made it through the hard times.

37. SKULLS

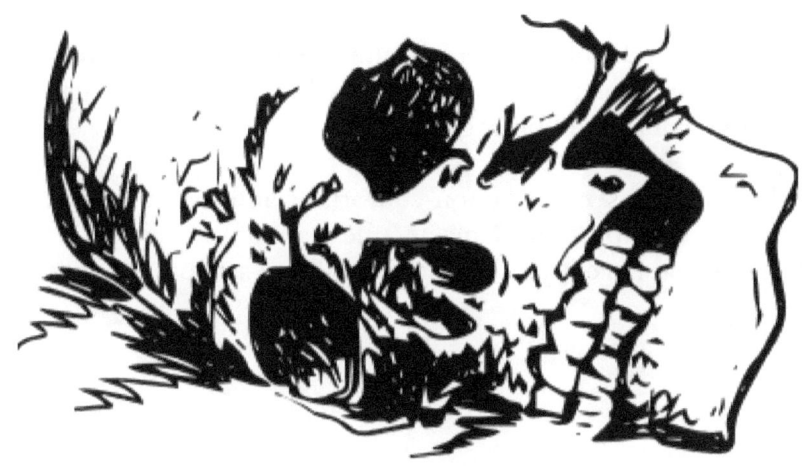

Once the reserve of bikers and just generally people who you wouldn't like to meet down a dark alley. The skull tattoo has firmly stood the test of time and come out the other side all the stronger.

When tattoos are mentioned, apart from maybe a mom heart or a rose, skulls are usually one of the first things people will think of. Certainly one of the all-time classics. If that isn't reason enough alone to justify getting a skull tattoo then I will lay some symbolism on you!

Now one thing I have to mention of course is sugar skulls. If you haven't heard of a sugar skull before, they were originally skulls made out of molded sugar and decorated. These sugar skulls would have the name of a departed loved one written on the forehead and then placed on their grave during the Day of the Dead Festival in Mexico.

Much of the meaning of sugar skull isn't taken into consideration by most people getting one as a tattoo, it's usually just the fact it's a nicely decorated skull that's appealing enough to make people want one. However if you did want to use the skull as a memorial tattoo then a name on the forehead is a great way to do that, or leave a space in preparation although that's quite morbid!

Skulls are a potent symbol of death for obvious reasons. This can add a variety of meanings to your tattoo. It could be as a reminder of our mortality or as a symbol of remembrance.

The skull is also definitely a very macho symbol and can represent toughness. The skull symbol has been used to evoke fear by groups such as the military and biker gangs.

The skull is also a symbol of non-conformity and sub-cultures. I wouldn't be able to begin to imagine the amount of heavy metal and rock bands that have used skulls in their album artwork at some point.

38. SNAKES

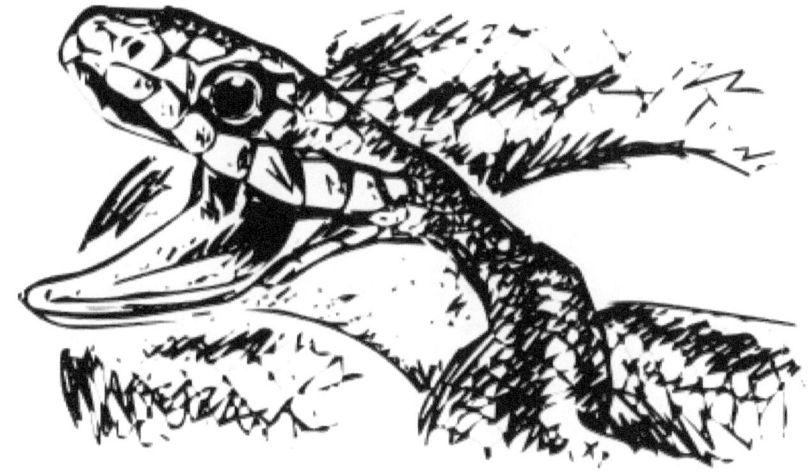

Snakes are another one of the all-time most iconic tattoo designs, especially when combined with a dagger on the forearm.

Snakes are symbolic of healing and renewing due to the way they shed their skin and emerge fresh and new. In many cultures they are associated with water which enforces this meaning due to waters healing and cleansing associations.

Throughout history dual snakes have been representative of balance and, in alchemy, the combining of two opposites in order to make something that is better than both of the parts. So dual snake tattoos can hold some great meaning too.

The snake has also been regarded as a symbol of protection. Many ancient cultures used the snake as a symbol to guard burial sites and their holy men would use the snake as a symbol as they were said to guard the higher mysteries.

Snakes are also a symbol of adaptability as with pretty much all types of reptile. Snakes can adapt to almost any environment from deserts to lakes and rivers. If you're the sort of person that can adapt to situations and make the best out of your circumstances then the snake tattoo might be just what you've been looking for.

Obviously snakes can't get away from the temptation meaning that they were lumped with by the old testament. So if you want a tattoo to represent resisting temptation or even glorifying temptation then a snake tattoo could be a good choice.

39. SPIDERS

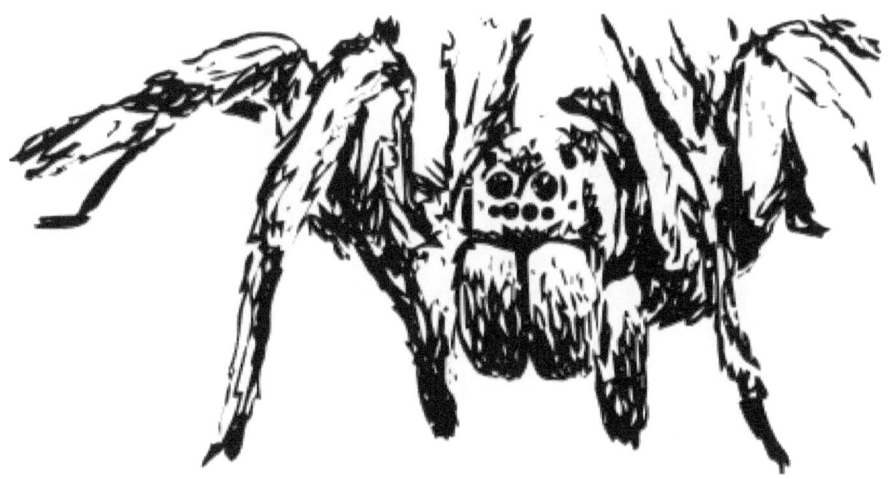

Spiders are obviously synonymous of fear and horror. I personally am not scared of spiders. That's probably because I live in England and we don't have any deadly ones but still, I don't find them scary and there must be a decent amount of people who share my opinion seeing as spider tattoos aren't uncommon these days.

The first piece of meaning that comes into my head is along the lines of the point I just mentioned. They may be small but they can strike fear into the hearts of something much bigger than them. Also, with spiders it seems that the smaller they are, the deadlier their venom is. This is a great metaphor for size not mattering in some sense.

If you look at the way we see spiders in general, it's not very nice. I mean as kids we hear nursery rhymes about a sider getting screwed over by the rain that keeps washing it down the water spout or that one about the spider that's creeping down on Little Miss Muffet. People also used to think the black plague was brought along by the spiders because they were working with the devil. It was of course not the siders at all and I think we should look at the good points.

Obviously as spiders are predatory creates that can be deadly even to humans, the sider associated with death and fear. They can also represent many other more respectable qualities however.

Spiders can represent resourcefulness. They can set up camp pretty much anywhere. It could be in a bush, inside your wing mirror or even in the corner of a room where there is almost no flies or anything to eat and they still do well!

Because of the way a spider will sit, waiting for their prey to come to them they can also represent patience and discipline.

40. SWALLOWS

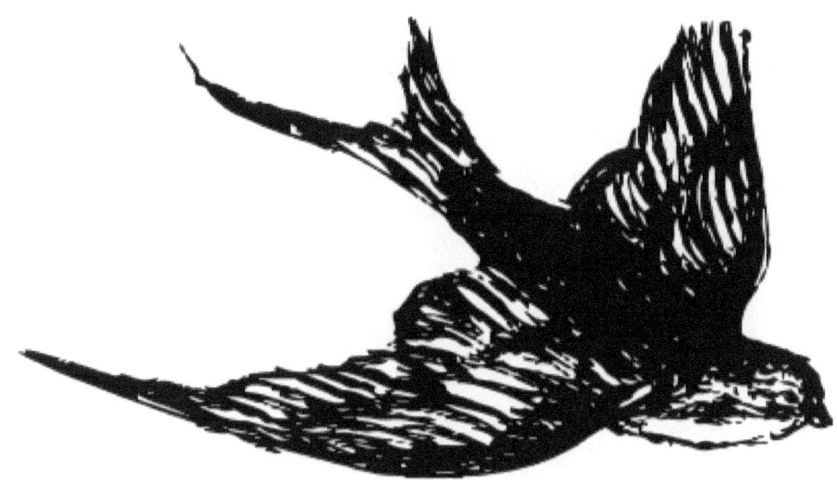

Another nautical tattoo, the swallow was commonly found on the arms of sailors.

The swallow tattoo is said to have been a British creation and based on the barn swallow. The story goes that if a sailor had a swallow tattoo it meant he has traveled at least 5000 nautical miles. It was considered to be a kind of badge of honor. Two swallows meant 10,000 nautical miles, so a real veteran!

Another more commonly known meaning behind the swallow tattoo is one of superstition. It was apparently thought that a swallow is a good luck symbol that would help ensure a sailors safe return home. This is commonly said to be because of the fact that if a sailor saw swallows then it meant they were reaching land. It's far more likely they would have seen a seagull to be fair so I doubt the legitimacy of that particular piece of reasoning. A more plausible reason is that the swallow actually returns to the same location every year to mate.

There's a little add on to this swallows returning to mate story that I found rather nice! In this version the sailor would get a single solitary swallow before they set off on their voyage. Then when they safely returned home they would get a second swallow as if the original swallow had returned and found its mate. If they didn't make it home however it was said that the swallow would take their soul to heaven.

As with most bird tattoos the swallow symbolizes freedom or spreading your wings and traveling somewhere new.

There's one final meaning that was created in Glasgow, Scotland that I find particularly charming! Apparently having a swallow on the back of your hand in this city back say 40-70 years ago meant "this fist flies". It was worn as a warning not to mess with them!

41. TIGERS

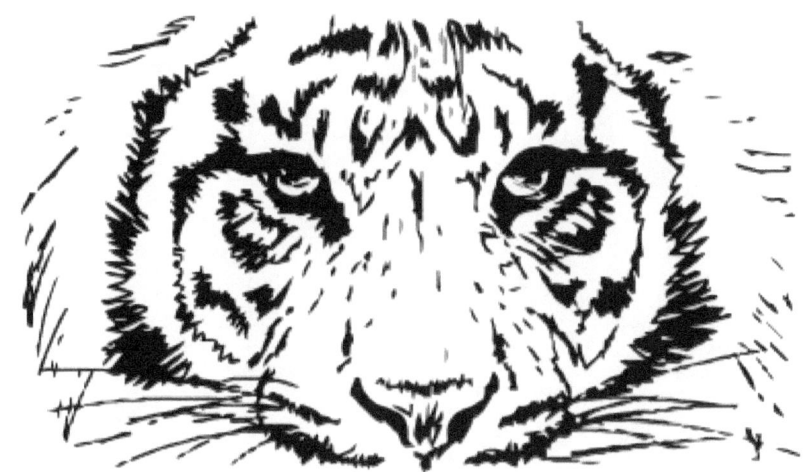

Nice to look at, strong, fearsome, skilled and graceful. No wonder the tiger was named one of the world's all-time favorite animals.

So the tiger is obviously representative of raw power due to its strong physical build. This can hold meaning in the sense of brute strength or this strength can be symbolically applied to anything you want really!

Now, I'm a Rocky fan and eye of the tiger was the perfect song to accompany the workout montage! But why was it called eye of the tiger? Because when the tiger stalks its prey it's focus and determination is unwavering. This meaning is great to apply to a tattoo too.

Tigers are often tattooed in the Japanese style and feature often in Japanese artwork in general.

In Chinese legend the universe is balanced by 5 tigers. Each of which are a different colour so we can find extra meaning in the colour of the tiger tattoo.

The white tiger rules autumn and governs the element, Metal. The black tiger rules over winter and water. The red tiger, you guessed it, rules summer and fire. The blue tiger rules spring and earth. The final tiger is yellow and it rules over the other 4 and keeps them in check.

42. WINGS

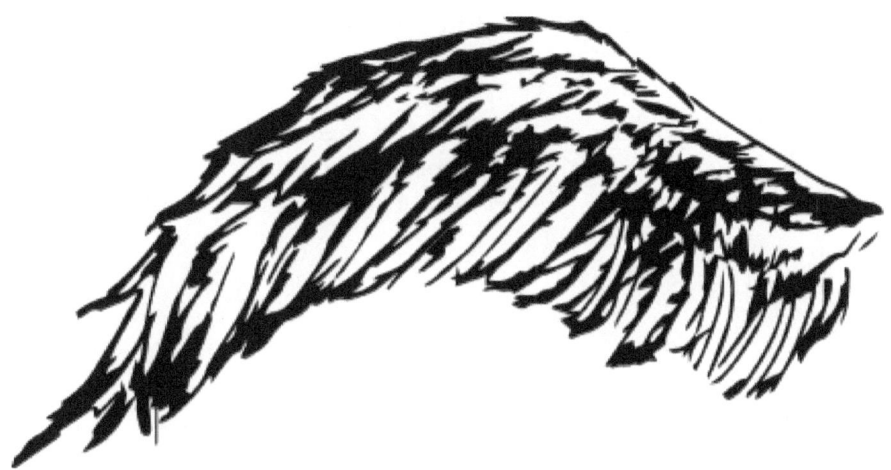

Wings are one of the only parts of an animal that is commonly tattooed without the rest of the animal present!

Wings are generally used to add meaning to another tattoo by adding a wing each side of whatever the design is. For example the winged heart tattoo is a popular one, I have also seen wings added to hour glasses or pocket watches to symbolize the fact that "time flies".

Now of course there is a lot of different types of wing, bird wings, bat wings, angel wings, butterfly wings, the list goes on. All of the different types of wing have some common symbolism.

Any type of wing can represent freedom, because of course, if you can fly you are far more free to travel wherever and whenever you want.

Wings also represent flight so can be used, as I mentioned earlier, to bring meaning to another tattoo such as the "time flies" example.

Wings are also a symbol of messengers. This is because of the way birds have been used to carry messages throughout history, but also because of the way ancient civilizations associated birds with being messengers of the gods.

Because of the messenger association, if you would like to add further meaning to your tattoo if it relates to receiving news be it good or bad or any other kind of message then wings are a great way to do this.

Wings are also symbolic of swiftness and speed as birds are able to cover great distances at surprising speeds but are also able to navigate in small spaces such as branches and bushes quickly and easily.

43. WOLVES

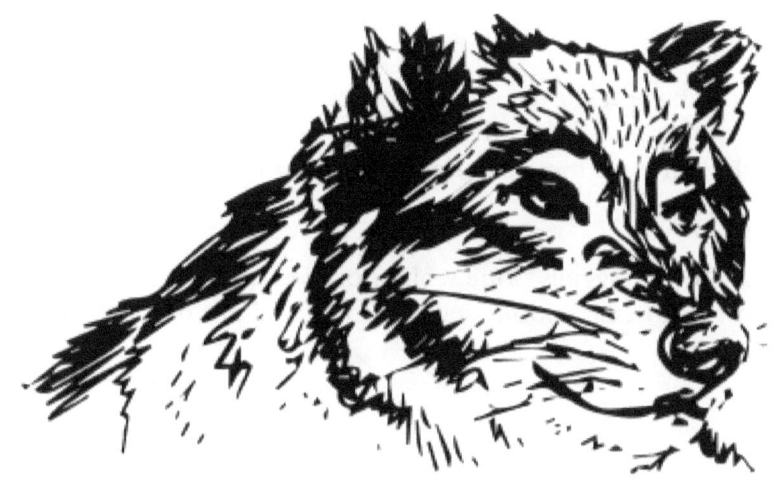

Wolves are fascinating creatures with a host of traits and behavioral traits that mean they sold a lot of symbolic meaning.

I think it's fair to say that early human interaction with wolves was a bit hit and miss and wolves would have been widely feared by the people ancient cultures. So much so in fact that the Greeks cooked up a crazy story, as they usually do, about a race of people who transformed into wolves once a year. This is where the legend of the werewolf comes from.

In the middle ages wolves were thought to be in cahoots with the Devil himself. This idea has stuck with those of us who descended from Christian ancestors and in fairytales and children's stories, the wolf is always bad.

Having said this though, those among you who know your stuff when it comes to ancient history will probably be thinking right now about the story of Romulus and Remus. If you don't know the story these two chaps were the founders of Rome, no biggie. They were raised and suckled by a she wolf. So if it wasn't for wolves, Rome would never have existed… that how the story goes at least.

The Romans may have liked the wolf a lot but, there was one culture who fully loved the wolf and they were of course the Native Americans. These guys saw the wolf as a totem of strength and also a strong spiritual symbol too.

Another thing you should know about wolves if you didn't already is that they mate for life and they are really good parents too. Combine this with their pack mentality and you have a fantastic symbol for loyalty and family.

There is also the saying "lone wolf" however, and a wolf tattoo could also represent being entirely self-sufficient and not needing the help of others.

44. FINAL THOUGHTS

Well, finally here we are at the end of my second book! This one too much longer than the first one but then it is twice the length. I really hope you enjoyed reading this and found some useful information.

If you did appreciate the book and you got it on Amazon or Kindle then I would hugely appreciate it if you could leave me a 5 star review and some kind words! It really does make such a difference to the sales that I get and every sale helps!

Thanks so much for reading this book and keep your eyes peeled for volume two, which depending on the reception this book gets in 2015 I may be writing. The 2nd book will have some slightly more obscure tattoo ideas in it as I covered pretty much all of the commonly tattooed designs in this book but I still think it may be worth writing.

Anyway, until next time, thanks for buying and reading! I really appreciate it!

TATTOO MEANINGS

GRAHAME DAVID GARLICK